'Nick's openness and honesty about his combined with his invaluable practical exactly what the world needs right now. mental health.'

Matt Eastwood, Global Chief Creative Officer,
McCann Health

'As is the case with others who have used life challenges as a spur for personal growth, Nick Bracks used his own deep insights into dealing with mental health challenges as inspiration for helping others who find themselves in the same situation. Nick draws on his own hard-won experience as well as pulling together key evidence, insights and advice from experts from many important fields. If you are seeking a life-changing road map to guide you to a path for improving your life and wellbeing then *Move Your Mind* is a go-to book.'

Dr Craig Hassed OAM

MOVE YOUR MIND

MOVE YOUR MIND

HOW TO BUILD A HEALTHY MINDSET FOR LIFE

NICK BRACKS

WILEY

First published in 2021 by John Wiley & Sons Australia, Ltd
42 McDougall St, Milton Qld 4064
Office also in Melbourne

Typeset in Plantin Std 11pt/16pt

ISBN: 978-0-730-39204-0

A catalogue record for this
book is available from the
National Library of Australia

Cover design by Wiley
Cover photo: © Andrew Raszevski

Disclaimer
The material in this publication is of the nature of general comment only, and does not represent professional advice. It is not intended to provide specific guidance for particular circumstances and it should not be relied on as the basis for any decision to take action or not take action on any matter which it covers. Readers should obtain professional advice where appropriate, before making any such decision. To the maximum extent permitted by law, the author and publisher disclaim all responsibility and liability to any person, arising directly or indirectly from any person taking or not taking action based on the information in this publication.

MIX
Paper from
responsible sources
FSC® C013604

CONTENTS

PREFACE

I've been fortunate to work as a mental health advocate for the past decade, which came about following my own personal battle with depression and anxiety. This experience has enabled me to work with leading wellness experts, travel around the globe and speak to people from all walks of life—young and old, privileged and poor.

As I began to lift back the layers, I saw that something was seriously missing. If daily life was becoming a struggle, where was the education that would help? Where were the tools to apply for a positive mindset? Add a global pandemic with anxiety and depression at record levels, and I questioned, what could be done on a *practical* level?

I wrote this book to fill that gap. To help you understand mental health in simple terms, and then move beyond that with a toolkit of practical daily techniques based on my experiences, learnings and expert insights. It was important to me that this book, like all the work I do in this area, also featured insights from experts, personalities and everyday people from all over the world. There's so much incredible knowledge out there and I've gone to great lengths to seek out the top thought leaders across many fields, such as psychologists, meditation and mindfulness experts, fitness professionals, doctors, advocates, sleep experts, nutritionists, philosophers and many more. It was also important to me that I spoke to personalities and everyday people and shared their stories. We learn from stories and by hearing about the trials and tribulations of these people we can find some common ground and realise that we're not alone and that we can overcome anything. You'll read insights from these experts, personalities and other inspirational people in the 'Insights' features scattered throughout the book. Many of them also share their habits, learnings and motivational tools—look out for sections headed 'Move Your Mind'.

I also share with you my own tools in the 'Move Your Mind with Nick' sections. The tools I share are ones I use in my own work, and they've proven successful for thousands of people around the world. If you can move your mind, you can master your inner world and live life on your terms.

I acknowledge that doing what is best for you is hard in the short term. It involves discipline and routine—things you may find confronting and challenging. While working through this book, remember that it's okay to be vulnerable. It's okay to cry, show emotion and not have all the answers when you want them. We're all human and we all feel things. It's okay to fail. Often, failure teaches us the biggest lessons in life. I don't want you to be like me when I was young: no tools, no knowledge, silently suffering.

Understand that there is always help—*always*—should you seek it. Make sure you have good people around you who you can check in with, and no matter how difficult things are, never neglect what keeps you happy and healthy, such as getting enough sleep, eating well, exercising, and seeing friends and loved ones. Remember that short-term discomfort will lead to long-term, sustainable health.

Push your ego aside and value your friends, family and those you come across in day-to-day life. Nurture them and treat people how you want to be treated. It's taken me my whole life to learn that true happiness comes from within, and until you can get off that treadmill (which I still often find myself on) you won't ever find peace.

Now more than ever, in our post-COVID world, you don't need more wealth, more validation or more social media 'likes'. You also don't need to be let down by a system that doesn't offer enough support—because seeking support can be too expensive and, ultimately, exhausting.

Like many before me, I've taken those hard-learned lessons and turned my life around. My mission is to make global change in mental health, recognising that we need to do more work as a society. I believe we need to embed education around mental health into the schooling system, into parenting, into universities and into businesses. I also think it should eventually be free, in much the same way as we can receive free treatment when we break a leg. It should be a fundamental part of what we get taught, and not just a resource for the elite few.

This book is divided into four parts. Part I sets the mental health landscape. You'll learn about the big picture: how mental health is affecting you, your children and economies around the world. Then, in part II, I break down mental health symptoms and conditions, and provide some examples of how I've worked with people on their journeys. This part of the book also gives some tips on starting the conversation about mental health.

In part III, I introduce you to my four practical pathways, which are the key to better mental health. Each one is designed to help you create preventative behaviours using real examples, tasks and stories to show you how others manage their challenges and conditions. Best of all, you can dip in and out of each one, taking what you need, when you need it.

Part IV brings it all together. It's the glue that packages up the learnings into long-term systems and habits so you can sustain the practical stuff and live your best life. You'll learn to use three actionable steps to train your mind and make lifelong changes. There are worksheets and tools you can use to put all the knowledge you collected in parts I to III into action—simply pick what speaks to you most. The worksheets can be downloaded, so you can use them again and again.

You have the power to make change yourself ... now. This is a book about self-love and guiding you to work on yourself. For those of you with mental health conditions—young people, older people, children, teachers, parents and everyone in between—I encourage you to find what will work for you within these pages. Use this book as a guide, an educational tool and a motivator to find your place while learning what options are available to you. This is just the beginning; it all starts now. If you're willing to put in the work, I'm ready to show you the way. Get ready to *Move Your Mind*!

ABOUT THE AUTHOR

Nick Bracks is a storyteller who has dedicated his adult life to creating positive conversations around mental health.

An acclaimed mental health advocate and successful multi entrepreneur, Nick has delivered 1,000+ mental health seminars around the globe, including two TED talks. This came about following his own personal and public battle with mental health and wellbeing.

Creative at heart, Nick is an actor with several films to his name and a two-year role on the well-loved Australian soap, *Neighbours*. Acting, along with exercise and meditation, is Nick's foundation for vibrant mental health.

Nick now spends his time advocating for mental health, speaking and interviewing, creating content and acting. His professional life and personal development are perfectly intertwined.

He lives between Australia and the United States.

ACKNOWLEDGEMENTS

Writing this book has been harder and more time consuming than I could have ever imagined...but, like most things that are challenging, it has been one of the most rewarding experiences of my life. It is the culmination of more than a decade of work as a mental health advocate, speaking more than 1,000 times all over the world; a varied career across the entertainment industry, along with starting multiple businesses; a lifetime of lessons learnt, experiences had and places travelled; and, most importantly, the amazing people I have met through the journey, from family, friends, collaborators, random encounters and everyone in-between.

There are too many people to personally thank but hopefully this does it justice.

A big thank you goes to all of the personalities and experts who were generous and kind enough to lend their time, knowledge and expertise (as you will read throughout the book). I am so fortunate to be able to connect and collaborate with such talented and inspiring people from all over the world. And a huge thank you to the Mental Health Charity One in Five for the ongoing support.

I would like to say thank you to Annie Reid from Atrium Media (www.atrium.media) for her incredible support and guidance in writing this book. I feel so lucky to have met and worked with her. She is an amazing person and someone I now consider a friend.

To my close friends (you all know who you are!) — thanks for always being there for me, supporting me and being unconditional. As you will read in the book, I feel very fortunate to have such an amazing support group. And a special thanks to Vincent De Luca and his extended network for the early support in this book.

I want to say a major thank you to Wiley for believing in me and publishing this book. They have been there every step of the way and have been an absolute joy to work with. They were the publisher I always wanted to work with and I couldn't have done it without them.

And finally to my family...

To my Mum, Terry and Dad, Steve—thank you for being the best parents in the world. Thank you for being amazing role models, teaching us about values and for genuinely being the best people I know.

To my brother and sister, Amy and Will, you are my best friends and the most genuine people I know. I wouldn't be who I am without you guys and am forever grateful for the relationship we have.

And to my extended family, again, I can't express how lucky I am to have such a loving and close family who support each other no matter what.

Finally, to Rob and Bruce, my Aunt and Uncle who are no longer with us, I dedicate this book to them. As you will read, they passed away during the formation of this book and have been my rock throughout life. They supported, pushed and encouraged me in every challenging endeavour I ever took on, were unconditional in their love and support and were always there for me. This book is for them.

INTRODUCTION

I just didn't know any better.

Time stopped, just like in the movies. I could see the houses in front of me as my car was spinning, and I could hear the song 'Under the Bridge' by Red Hot Chili Peppers at full blast. I remember thinking quite clearly, 'This could be the end', and having a wave of emotions crash over me. My heart sank.

It was a cold, rainy night on 13 July 2007, on the back of a big week of partying. My parents were away at our family holiday house in Wye River, Victoria, and I had a group of friends staying over at my home in Williamstown, Melbourne. We'd been out drinking on consecutive nights and, apparently, I'd been drinking everyone else under the table that week. Always the dedicated obsessive: if I was going to drink, I was going to do the job properly.

That night, we'd been out drinking again at Seven Nightclub at a night called 'Unlucky Thursdays'. It was our favourite and I looked forward to it all week. Drunk after another big session, I finished up and left, along with my best friend, Huw, and mates Aidan and Jason. We took a taxi and headed back to my house.

Once home, I don't know what had possessed me to get into the family Saab. Maybe I wanted to grab some food. I can't be sure. Huw, who I'd grown up with, decided to jump into the car with me. He was in a similar drunken state, and for some reason decided to lie down across the back seats of the car.

I took off, flying down the main street in Williamstown at 90 km/h in a 60 zone, screaming the lyrics to that song. Then, something clicked in my head and I realised what I was doing and what was happening in that moment, and I knew it was very dangerous.

I instantly tried to turn the car around to head home, and I remember the feeling as it happened. Everything was in slow motion and my life flashed before my eyes. It was just like you'd see in a movie. As I wrenched the steering wheel, the car hit a traffic island and started spinning out of control. I could see the houses in front of me as the car continued to spin, only stopping because it slammed into a tree, completely crushing in one side—the side Huw's head was facing as he lay down.

I was stunned, and for several moments after the car finally stopped, I sat there gripping the steering wheel and breathing hard. I ripped the cassette player out to make it stop playing.

With my seatbelt on, I miraculously suffered no injuries beyond a bit of whiplash. Dazed, I looked over my shoulder at the back seats. Huw was lying across the seats, covered in blood and dangerously still. I called out to him, but he didn't answer. Ripping off my seatbelt, I turned, shouting his name again and again to no response.

Finally, he twitched, shook his head and sat up. I was enormously relieved to discover that he was alive, and not at all surprised to find that he was completely shell-shocked.

Had he not had a reflex to jolt up, he would have been killed instantly. But somehow, he seemed relatively okay, and despite being covered in blood with gashes in his arm and face, decided to walk home, which was a few kilometres away. He hoped it would save me from getting into more trouble.

By this point I knew I was in trouble. People were running out of their houses, and I ended up asking them if I could call the police because I wanted to handle the situation myself. When they arrived, they took me willingly to the police station, from where I had to make one of the hardest phone calls of my life. It was to my dad, Steve Bracks, the premier of Victoria at the time. After I explained what had happened, his and my mum's main concern was our wellbeing. It was now 7 am and I was told my incident would be all over the news by 8 am that morning.

At 8 am, it became a national story. I couldn't leave the house for days because media were camped out the front. Bizarrely, one of the main photos that appeared was of the written-off car in a junk yard with a black cat sitting on top of it. Our night out at 'Unlucky Thursdays' seemed very apt.

I remember telling myself at this time that I had to make a change, that I was going to stop drinking, and had to make a plan to get myself on track. Enough was enough. I'd been given a second chance. The police who were at the scene of the incident said they had never seen one that severe where anyone had survived. I was lucky to be alive, and even more so, was lucky I didn't kill my best friend or harm anyone else.

Furthermore, I had brought my family front and centre into the wreckage that was my mind and body, and it was time to see the signals and make a change. I stuck to this for a couple of weeks, but because

I was still not willing to talk openly about what had happened and seek the help that I needed, I quickly fell back into the same behaviour patterns and regularly found myself in life-threatening situations.

I think the car crash was when my bad-boy image was born. After the story came out, I found myself the centre of attention, and people were watching every move I made. As long as I was drunk, though, I didn't mind. I felt like I could get away with anything.

The weird part was that I wasn't famous for being an amazing football player or an Olympian or an actor. I'd done nothing more than crash a car. Looking back, I realise now that I was very naïve and stupid, but at the time I thought it was fun to get into nightclubs without having to pay the cover charge. I loved the approval from crowds of people I didn't even know. During this time, going out was my world.

Even then, I could see that things had taken a seriously wrong turn in my life, but I couldn't see that I had bigger issues to tackle than just the drinking—alcohol had been nothing more than a really bad coping mechanism for some serious problems.

I just didn't know any better.

PART I

MENTAL HEALTH AND WELLBEING

The impact of mental health on people and economies worldwide is devastating. Approximately one billion people globally suffer from a mental health disorder, and lost productivity from untreated mental health disorders costs the global economy US$1 trillion each year.

My life's purpose is to see global reform around mental health systems and for people to prioritise their own mental health above all else.

In part I, I'll share my own challenges with mental health issues and the simple go-to I use to manage them. With the help of two mental health experts, I'll discuss what mental illness is and how we can educate young people in particular to identify their own mental health issues and to seek help. I'll also impart some solid strategies for coping with mental health challenges.

FEAR IS IMPORTANT BECAUSE IT LEADS TO HAPPINESS.

FAILURE IS IMPORTANT BECAUSE IT LEADS TO SUCCESS.

CHAPTER 1
MY STORY

As a young kid, I always wanted to be the centre of attention, trying to do the most extreme acts I could think of and always pushing the boundaries. I was incredibly active, which, even as a little kid, was a way to cope with putting my overactive mind at bay. It's incredibly unpleasant to have compulsive thoughts, and trying to ignore them or push them away doesn't always work.

One of the earliest stories I remember is my obsession with Gary Ablett Senior, an iconic player in the AFL. My dream as a kid was to play AFL and he was the pinnacle, arguably one of the greatest players of all time, who played for the team I had grown up supporting—the Geelong Football Club.

I remember once heading to one of our family holiday house trips at Wye River and stopping in Geelong to visit a sports store. In the corner of the store, I spotted him—Gary Ablett—and instantly froze. My dad offered to approach him and introduce him to me, but I was so overwhelmed by the situation that I ran and hid in the change rooms, refusing to come out, not reappearing until Dad assured me Gary had left.

For the next month all I would talk about was how devastated I was with myself about passing up an opportunity to meet my hero. It ate away at me. More comically, and not long after this incident, I was in religion class at school and we were asked to draw a picture of God. Very seriously, I drew a picture of Gary Ablett kicking a goal in football.

A few weeks later, my uncle took me to a Geelong game at the then Optus Oval, a football ground. We were sitting on the forward line and in the final stages of the last quarter I saw Gary Ablett kick up a chunk of grass. As soon as I saw it, I became fixated on acquiring this piece of grass. When the siren sounded, I was over the fence, weaving through security to grab the grass that Gary Ablett's boot had kicked up. Luckily, I was able to pick up the grass before I was escorted off the ground. I carefully took it home, planted it and would water it every day. I would get up before my parents each morning, sit on the windowsill, eat a piece of this grass and pray that it would make me as good at football as Gary Ablett. If only life were that simple!

This compulsive behaviour wasn't a one-off. It manifested in many ways during my adolescence and caused me incredible difficulty in my developmental years.

As I mentioned, I quickly became obsessed with the idea of playing AFL football, to the point of training six hours a day as an 11-year-old. I don't know exactly why I felt this urge, and I didn't really question it. I didn't have the self-awareness or life experience to understand it. But it was overwhelming and strong, and I didn't feel I had a choice. I simply had to do it—like a never-ending pit that I just couldn't pour enough fuel into.

The issue was that I was incredibly shy and insecure, and this only added to my need to prove I was more capable in sport than anyone around me by pushing myself to the limit. It was a way of compensating for my combination of introversion, with a need to perform and express myself by physically doing extreme things. In doing so, I could express and give an outlet to what was going on in my mind, with sport being the manifestation.

Perhaps this was fuelled even further by having a well-known and successful father. By the time I turned 12 he had become the premier of Victoria—a position he maintained until my early 20s. I was and always have been proud of him, but I think it added fuel to an already burning fire to prove myself and achieve big things. I have no doubt I would have behaved in this way regardless, but it became a combination of nature and nurture driving my extreme behaviour.

I can vividly remember getting up at 2.30 am to exercise at the age of 12. My parents could see I was showing very unhealthy and obsessive behaviour patterns. And as with most addictions, I felt extreme shame and guilt about it and would do my best to hide things from them. Mum had to take my mini weights and equipment off me to put a stop to my obsessive training.

But that didn't stop me. I would go out into the backyard and sneak bricks into my room. I would hide them under my bed, or anywhere I could, and use them to secretly train. I would do a range of exercises for around three hours with the bricks; then, when I heard Mum get up at 6.30 am, I would pretend I had just woken up and head out for a one-and-a-half-hour run before school.

Sometimes, when parliament was sitting, Dad would get home late. I can remember being up and starting my training just as Dad was arriving home at 2 am. It was totally illogical, unhealthy and extreme, but I simply didn't know how to stop.

At this point, I was also training to become a middle-distance runner, and had become so fit through all my training for football that I would win every distance competition. After completing my 2.30 am morning training, I would go to school and go straight from there to that night's training, often tripling what my coach had set for me. For example, my night training would be a 30–45-minute warm-up jog, followed by 20 × 400-metre sprints at 80 per cent with a 400-metre jog in between for recovery. I remember getting home and being so tired that I wasn't able to even walk upstairs to take myself to bed. This behaviour went on for years.

Because of my fixation and obsession, I didn't develop socially and isolated myself from other people through my entire high school years (other than close friends I had known throughout my adolescence). I felt even more of an outcast as the level of training was clearly having an impact on my physical development.

By the age of 16, I was yet to hit puberty. I had punished my body to such a degree for so many years that I had stunted my physical development. Among many issues that this caused was a delay in my performance as an athlete. I still got the results, but on the running track and on the football field, I simply couldn't compete with 16-year-olds who had the bodies of men when I was still built like a 12-year-old.

It caused me to distance myself from others throughout my entire high school years, especially girls. I was embarrassed, ashamed and disgusted with myself for not fitting in and developing as I should have. I would pray every night, begging for my body to grow and develop as it should. It was extremely confusing and frustrating. It planted insecurities and stories in my head that I am still undoing to this day.

By the time I finished high school, my body had broken down. My extreme training had caused patella tendonitis, among other knee problems, and I had no other choice than to stop training. I tried everything, obsessively doing hours of rehab each day, but nothing could undo the damage I had done. I remember my sister telling me of the screaming and crying that would come out of my room. It was utter grief and helplessness. My vice had been taken away. The only thing I placed my self-worth on was gone. I wasn't coping and simply didn't see a future if I couldn't be a professional athlete.

By this point in time, to my relief, my body had finally started to grow. I went from being 150 centimetres at 16 and built like a 12-year-old, to nearly 180 centimetres by the time I turned 19. It seems that growth was to come late in all aspects of my life, not only my physical development, which continued into my 20s.

I had also just discovered alcohol around this time. Alcohol gave me the confidence to be myself, speak my mind, interact socially and forget my problems. But unfortunately, this only created bigger problems, as you'll read later.

Realising I had a problem

After high school, I deferred from university and took a gap year. I had no idea what I wanted to do but had been accepted into a double degree of Commerce and Health Promotion at Deakin University. The gap year was a good experience in leaving Australia and experiencing something different, but it was also problematic.

I was incredibly insecure and shy and found it very difficult to interact with others. I would spend a lot of time alone, hiding away trying not to be seen. I was able to travel around a lot of Europe with Huw (who was later in the car crash I talked about in the introduction to the book) and spent a lot of time drinking and using it to mask my discomfort with not knowing how to cope on my own. For the most part, I struggled. Towards the end of the year, my dad had his third election approaching, and due to my struggles, I decided to come home and be there for it.

I started my course at Deakin only to pull out after just six weeks. I was too depressed and couldn't bring myself to try to fit in and meet people. This only led to further alcohol abuse, where I would build my whole week around it. I wasn't working or doing anything else, just counting down the time until I could drink again.

I would be out every Thursday, Friday and Saturday night, and often many other nights, drinking myself into the ground. For me, that same compulsion that I had when it came to competing in sport would kick in. I loved the feeling of escape; I loved the complete freedom my mind gave me to fully express myself, say what I thought and show my personality. I would push myself for no reason other than to outdrink whoever was around me, fuelled by a compulsion that felt illogical but, again, that I couldn't help.

The short-term high of this behaviour would lead to incredible lows. I'd spend the week in bed, locked under the covers, afraid to face the outside world. It also led to life-threatening incidents on a weekly basis. I would wind up passing out in random places, vomiting all over myself, walking down freeways against traffic and making dangerous decisions.

Around that time, I began seeing a psychologist, and also told one of my close friends about what I had been going through. At this point I hadn't told anyone else. I was even too embarrassed to tell my parents how I felt, despite them seeing me fall apart and facilitating the psychologist. I was literally trembling, thinking that my friend would never look at me in the same way again.

But to my surprise it was the complete opposite—she understood, offered emotional support and was there for me. It was a major weight off my shoulders and was the beginning of me eventually talking to more people about it. Importantly, reaching out for the first time instilled in me a key point I regularly speak about now: the importance of having unconditional relationships.

Meanwhile, I was still dealing with issues around drinking and abusing alcohol and had major insecurities and hang-ups from growing up. One of those was around girls. I hadn't been with many girls until the age of 19, when I had my first sexual experience with someone 10 years older than me. It was a relief to have finally had the experience, but due to the social isolation and shame that I felt through my adolescence about not fitting in, I had enormous insecurity about being vulnerable or intimate with girls. I relied on alcohol to interact and turned down opportunity after opportunity to date girls who showed interest in me. I had an irrational fear that I couldn't explain and allowed it to hinder me from having the experience I wanted most: to be in a relationship.

Getting help

For years, I had been suffering and done too little about it. I would come up with every excuse possible to avoid being vulnerable and confronting these issues. I knew that things would not magically get better, but I was afraid of my own shadow and too scared to do anything about it. I was also becoming more self-destructive and didn't see a way out; nor did I want a way out as I felt I had nothing left that I cared about.

It got to a point where I couldn't leave my bed even to do something as simple as walk downstairs and wash the dishes. I was almost catatonic. I couldn't hide the severity of what I was experiencing from my family either, and finally my mum intervened. She dragged me to a psychologist to get the help I so desperately needed. I was now 20 years old.

It was during my first session with the psychologist that I found out I was severely depressed. Even after all I had been through, it still came as a shock. I saw depression as something I was stronger than and thought it was embarrassing for a man to fall victim to such a thing.

But this feeling very quickly turned to relief as I was shown examples of people who had been through similar things and had come out okay at the other end. I began to understand why it was happening to me, to be able to own up to my story and then start to move beyond making plans and begin to make changes.

I found this incredibly liberating. When you're in such a state, often no amount of reasoning or logic will change your mind. You feel so overwhelmed that the thought of facing the future is simply untenable to you. I felt like my life was over and so riddled with emotional pain that no words could describe what it felt like.

Now, it really scares me to think back to those times where I had lost all hope. But equally, I'm thankful that I experienced them and forever grateful I have such a close-knit family and friends who love me. I know now that if I hadn't experienced all of this, I wouldn't be able to develop the same level of empathy for others who were suffering.

It also taught me to never judge, to always listen and never compare two situations. Everyone has their own story, and everyone's suffering is relevant under their given circumstances. The key is taking action before things become bigger and bigger problems.

Beginning to heal

As part of my healing, I enrolled in a Business and Entrepreneurship course at RMIT University. After so long out of university and not working, I needed some purpose and something to focus on. The psychologist was instilling in me the importance of taking baby steps forward, so I liked the sound of starting my own business. But there was a hurdle: I was expected to do 15 oral presentations in the first semester as part of the assessment.

I was still too shy to speak in front of even one person, and couldn't look people in the eye, so I completely panicked. I couldn't sleep, was sick to my stomach and tried to pull out of the course due to my fear of public speaking. I would have quit too had I not had the support of my mum, the psychologist and my friend. They knew, as I did, that pulling out would not only waste more time, but would also lead to having no purpose again and putting myself in life-threatening situations.

I turned up for the first of the presentations. They were often in front of just five people, as it was a small course. Nonetheless, I was in a state of sheer panic. So much so that I vomited in the bathroom beforehand.

When it came time to deliver the presentation, I read what I had written word for word and stood there, staring at the floor and mumbling the words. No-one would have understood anything that I said. As horrendous as I felt, nothing bad happened. Sure, I'd made a terrible job of that first speech, but I'd kept going and got through it, even when I stuffed up.

I did many more like that and they taught me an invaluable lesson: *not to listen to all the stories that your mind tells you*. My mind would say, 'Nick, you're not good enough', 'You are pathetic', 'You have nothing good to say' and 'You don't deserve to be here' to the point where I would throw up beforehand. We can't stop our mind from thinking, but we can choose which thoughts we give power to.

As well as not listening to the stories your mind tells you, it also taught me something I apply to this day: *not to give credit to everything your mind tells you.* It taught me that even when I did an average job, people were supportive. It taught me that it's okay to try new things and that it's okay to not be the best. The only way anyone gets good at anything is by taking that first step. I use this mindfulness technique to this day.

By the end of that course at university, I was comfortable speaking in front of groups of people and had made major progress in my mental health. I had also started to develop a passion for mental health and helping others, which sowed the first seeds of my work in this area.

Getting the word out

Around this time, I had been approached by modelling agencies and was regularly appearing in the media, social circuit and getting booked for modelling jobs. I think this gave people the idea that I was someone I was not. While I had made some self-improvement, the reality was that I was still scared and insecure and had no self-love. I was afraid of being myself and was desperately hoping for more attention, fame or admiration to justify my existence. It wasn't until my late 20s that I finally experienced a relationship. I had so desperately wanted it for so long but had never allowed it to happen. I always told myself no-one was good enough, but the reality was that I didn't feel like I was good enough.

Then one day, I was invited to appear on the reality show *Dancing with the Stars*. Immediately, my competitive side kicked in and I said yes, also thinking that I could raise awareness and money for a charity I believed in (I wanted to help in mental health).

But I woke up the next morning in a cold sweat thinking, 'What the f*ck have I just said yes to!?' I couldn't even dance when I was out with a group of friends, let alone in front of a live audience on live television broadcast around the country to more than three million people. I panicked and tried to pull out, before reminding myself of my experience with public speaking, and how it changed my life. I thought if I could get through that, then maybe this was possible too, and that I may learn something about myself along the way.

To this day, I was more nervous than I have ever been in my life on the first episode of that show. I was probably one of the worst dancers in the history of the show, but I survived it, and ended up staying in until week seven of 10. I was also able to speak out about my own mental health publicly for the first time. More importantly, it was this that led me to being invited to speak in schools and share my story. Had I not overcome my fear of public speaking I wouldn't have been able to do the show and I would have missed the opportunity that changed my life.

In those first school talks, I quickly saw the impact of simply speaking openly and authentically. Kids would come up and tell me it led to them getting help for the first time. It sparked something in me, and in the years since I have spoken more than 1000 times both in Australia and overseas, at schools, universities, companies, in the media, even doing two TEDx talks. It led to working with behaviour-change companies, charities, individuals and eventually starting my own seminar company and producing video and audio programs around mental wellbeing. My goal is simple: to make global change in mental health by whatever means are available to me.

Fulfilling my purpose and passion

Following *Dancing with the Stars*, I launched my first business, an underwear label called underBRACKS. At the time, I was booking a lot of underwear modelling work, had just finished my degree and wanted to start my own business. After all the media attention from being on television, people joked that I should start my own underwear label. Eventually I thought, why not? I did it on a whim and learned and made mistakes as I went along. We sold them online and eventually did a deal with retailer Myer. It was a really valuable first foray into the business world. Since then, I've opened a café in Melbourne's CBD called The Lobby 601, co-founded a nutrition company, started a wellness app called Happy Waves, and launched the Move Your Mind organisation and podcast, of which I'm very proud.

I moved into acting following the reality shows (I was also on a show called *Celebrity Splash*) with a completely misguided idea in my mind that I could become famous. Once I started attending acting classes, that thought was quickly dispelled and I ended up falling in love with the process of simply doing it.

I did years of classes, at one point full time, and slowly began to grow more self-love and self-awareness as well as developing a clear focus and goal in my life. My goal to make global change in mental health was joined by another one: to land acting work. To be a good actor, you must understand yourself, get over your ego and have an open mind as to why people behave as they do. You have to learn not to judge and really understand what drove someone to become the person they are. It all resonated so clearly with me and I think acting is one of the best things you can do for personal development. It certainly has become something that continues to ground me and keep me focused on my work.

As a result, I was lucky enough to land a role on the iconic Australian television program *Neighbours* on and off for two years. I have since been cast in an Australian feature film and moved to Vancouver and the United States to audition for American roles. Regardless of whether it takes off as a career, I know I'll always act for myself.

It's become a passion and I really believe that purpose and passion are two of the most important things for your mental health. If you have a daily purpose and are doing things you are passionate about, then the end goal doesn't matter. The only thing you can ever control is what you do right now, so not enjoying the process amounts to not enjoying life. All you ever have is right now.

Facing fear and failure

At this stage, I felt like my life was finally on track. I was starting the new app business with a great team and investors on board. I was getting comfortable with acting, *Neighbours* was going well and I was also in a two-year relationship and in love for the first time in my life.

But within two weeks, a chain of events completely out of my control knocked me for six. Things abruptly ended with my girlfriend, and one of my businesses was in turmoil. Despite spending two years creating the company, putting everything I had into it and launching it successfully, there was an internal issue out of my control that caused the business to break down.

Suddenly, I was seeing years of my work go down the drain. Plus, I was dealing with my first heartbreak. I felt like it was going to break me and I didn't know where to turn or what to do. I was losing hope and finding it difficult to overcome the emotional pain.

But rather than hide from the feelings and block them out, I decided to draw on what I had previously learned and embrace them. Yes, I felt like I'd lost control of everything, but I wanted to feel all the pain and use the time to reflect. So, I drew on my daily habits by embracing my exercise, meditation and alone time—things that were all fully in my control.

I started small, took baby steps and focused on the process. Gradually things got better and I found that I grew in ways I didn't think I would. For example, I can safely say if I hadn't had the daily habit of exercising, I wouldn't have been able to make it through that period in a sane manner. I knew that no matter how bad the day was (and most were bad), I could exercise at least once every single day. And I knew that this would always put my mind at ease, allow me an hour or so of not thinking about anything other than moving, and, without a shadow of a doubt, leave me feeling emotionally and physically significantly better than when I began. This experience really reinforced just how important exercise (and other daily habits) are in our daily wellbeing.

Now, as I write this book, I look back on the car crash, the humiliation and all the dangerous situations I've put myself in, and I believe it's essential to face fears and go through pain to grow. Until you can learn to live with discomfort, I don't believe you can be the best version of yourself.

A final word

Fear is important because it leads to happiness. Failure is important because it leads to success. You need to look at failure not as failure but as learning. If you can reframe your mindset to see two possible outcomes when approaching a new task—I will either learn something (instead of viewing it as failure) or I will achieve my goal—then you'll be in a better mindset and more willing to take risks and grow. I tell myself that it will be uncomfortable at the beginning but if I can stick to it, things will get easier. And they always do. Once you can grasp this, you'll become so much better equipped to improve yourself.

There's no right or wrong way to go about anything and you need to learn to trust yourself, to trust your gut. Everyone has an opinion and they're often projecting their own insecurities onto you when offering advice. If you can simplify things and work out what you value, what you're passionate about and what you want to dedicate each day to doing, then the rest will work itself out.

Remember that you can't control what will happen in the future, but you can control what you decide to do and where you want to put your attention right now—and that's all you can ever control.

TO MAKE LONG-TERM CHANGE WE NEED TO SKILL UP YOUNG PEOPLE AND GIVE THEM THE PRACTICAL SKILLS TO DEAL WITH ISSUES AS THEY COME UP.

Brydie Huggins

CHAPTER 2

UNDERSTANDING MENTAL HEALTH

When I was growing up, I didn't really know what mental health was. All I knew was that I had extreme thinking that would manifest in different ways.

From as far back as I can remember, I overthought everything with a running commentary in my head that never turned off. I can also see that I had OCD issues and obsessive thoughts, which, looking back, completely ruled my life.

It's important to understand that these intrusive thoughts can be related to all things, big and small. Sometimes it becomes a fixation about big things such as the obsession with competing in sport. But often the fixation can arise around more trivial things, such as buying an item of clothing or getting a new computer. I can remember obsessing about purchasing a new laptop. My previous one was worn out and I had to buy a new version, the latest model. The new computer was slightly bigger but still completely portable, and better in every way. Rather than enjoying the convenience of this I began obsessing that it was not as small as my past laptop and that it would be too big to carry around. I panicked, trying to return it and desperately called around asking if they still had the old version in stock. This went on for weeks until I eventually got used to the new computer. Looking back, it was an utterly pointless and ridiculous thing to obsess about. But I can remember many similar examples, all of which made no logical sense. The point here is that the thinking patterns are usually not about the actual item or event itself, but more so about a deeper issue or habit that needs to be reconditioned.

Again, I didn't know any differently. I didn't have the self-awareness, knowledge or openness to question what was going on in my head all the time. So I suffered in silence, like so many others.

My life's purpose today is to effect global changes in mental health. It's taken all my life to get to this point, and while I never imagined as a kid that this would be my path, I'm very proud to stand up and say that it is.

Mental health is a global epidemic. Poor mental health is the leading source of disability around the world, with depression being the leading cause. Specifically, depression and anxiety cost the global economy one trillion US dollars every year.

One trillion! That's a big figure—a million million—that's the number 1 followed by 12 zeros. I can't even wrap my head around it. Globally right now, there are more than 300 million people suffering from depression.

In Australia, untreated mental health issues cost Australian businesses at least $10.09 billion per year. According to a 2012 study by US publication *Scientific American* titled 'The Neglect of Mental Illness Exacts a Huge Toll, Human and Economic', untreated mental illnesses cost more than $100 billion per year in lost productivity. Even scarier, mental health issues will cost the world US $16 trillion by 2030. It's a huge problem, and it affects people from all walks of life—from poverty to privilege.

Key learnings

Poor mental health is now the leading cause of disability worldwide, with more than 300 million people suffering from depression. Here are some facts:

1. Globally, one person commits suicide every 40 seconds.

2. Depression and anxiety cost the global economy around one trillion US dollars each year.

3. Depression is the leading cause of disability worldwide.

What is mental health?

The World Health Organization (WHO) defines mental health as:

A state of wellbeing in which every individual realises his or her own potential, can cope with the normal stresses of life, can work productively and fruitfully, and is able to make a contribution to their community.

For me, the key focus is the first four words: 'a state of wellbeing'. Breaking it down further, it's the word 'state'. A state is a condition, or a mode of being. It's not static, but rather a fluid motion that is moving. Therefore, I see mental health as a continuum that moves between various states, ranging from mentally unwell to mentally healthy.

As a kid, teenager and young adult, I remember being in varying states of mental health. Sure, there were great days, but there was always the running commentary and the extreme compulsion for whatever my chosen coping mechanism was at the time—whether that was sport or alcohol.

Today, as a much healthier and happier person, I manage the compulsive behaviours through healthy habits and routine. There are some days where I'm up, and some days where I'm down. Some days

I don't have all the answers, and that's okay. It's more normal to have ups and downs than to be happy all the time.

By framing mental health as a moving state, you can strip it back so that it's easy to understand. And that's what we want to try to do here, because if something is easier to understand, it's so much easier to manage.

Another way to look at it is that mental health needs to be viewed in the same way as a broken arm: if you break your arm you go and see a doctor. If you have a problem in your mind, you should go and seek help in exactly the same way because these are both common problems that can be managed and fixed.

One of the things I always say is that it's okay to not be okay. In fact, it's perfectly normal. It's more abnormal to go through life without having any mental health–related problems. So, when it comes to your mental health, there's only one thing you should never do—*nothing*. Let me repeat this, there is only one thing you should never do—*nothing*. The longer you leave it, the bigger the problem will become.

The first step is about just doing something, whether that be calling a friend, speaking to a professional, taking some time out or calling a free anonymous help line (these can be found by typing 'anonymous helpline' into Google).

Never wait and hope things will get better. If you're suffering, do something. It may be venting to a friend or it may be getting professional help. The longer you let it manifest, the harder it will be to deal with. Get on top of it now.

What is mental illness?

Mental illness refers to a range of mental health conditions and disorders that affect mood, thinking and behaviour. A few of the main symptoms include addictive behaviours, depression, anxiety disorders, eating disorders, suicide, burnout and overwhelm. I'll cover these in more detail later, but for now, the defining factor between normal functionality in everyday life with some occasional mental health concerns and having a mental health issue is when ongoing signs and symptoms often cause stress and the inability to function properly each day.

A mental illness can start to affect everything—including school, work, parenting, sport and socialising—and lead to problems such as taking drugs, excessive drinking and relationship breakdowns.

Where do mental health and illness stem from?

Historically, mental health issues have been judged and hidden by society. When they're hidden, they're swept under the carpet, managed privately and discreetly. When they're out in the open, they're judged, often harshly.

The judging ranges from assertions of being 'weak', 'lazy', 'anti-social' or 'making excuses', which, along with feelings of guilt, unworthiness and self-judgement, perpetuates the stigma and silence that struggles may be met with.

But staying silent means that mental health stays untreated, and unnoticed. This causes damage to families and communities, and contributes to the further stigmatisation of mental health. That's why it's so important that we all get better at speaking up and reducing the damage. We know that talking openly and honestly about mental health helps to reduce the stigma that causes people to suffer privately. And by talking about mental health problems and being open to finding support, the whole community benefits.

Today, there's much more coverage on the positive aspects of mental health. There's better coverage in the media, better mental health literacy and even royal commissions looking into the mental health system. There are simply not enough prevention measures in place and the government is now realising this.

Some of the more popular awareness events include 'R U OK Day', which is run by a suicide prevention charity, as well as 'Movember', which has been super successful in supporting men's health since it was launched in 2003. I have worked with Movember several times over the years, speaking and engaging in different initiatives, and have always been impressed with their work.

Youth mental health

Whether it's rushing off to get to the next thing, keeping up with the Joneses or looking at a screen, there's a lot of pressure, particularly on young children and adolescents, to perform and keep up with the world. You're not alone if you think there's something a bit amiss in society at the moment. Everyone seems to be so busy!

The truth is that kids are growing up with technology, and it's having a huge impact on their mental health. The nature of life right now is fast paced, with greater pressure on young people to succeed academically, socially and athletically. Plus, with the increased exposure to media and screens, and a tendency to compare themselves with what they see on social media, young people are experiencing higher levels of stress than ever before.

This sets up a falsely idealised 'reality' where kids are comparing the behind-the-scenes of their lives with the highlight reel of what's presented in someone else's life on social media. And they're looking at that and wondering, 'What's wrong with my life? Why doesn't mine match up with theirs?'

When I was growing up, we would sit down together as a family almost every night for dinner. I can see now how important that is.

The scary thing is that we don't know how difficult this is going to become in the future because we've never had to deal with it before. Kids are growing up using platforms such as Facebook, TikTok and Instagram, and these platforms are just as addictive as substances prohibited to kids such as alcohol or drugs.

Every time they get a 'like', it releases dopamine in the brain, and that connection creates a very unhealthy addiction to these platforms. It's the same connection created through drug and alcohol abuse, but because it's currently unregulated for teens, they can use it as much as they like. Screen time and social media usage are also unprecedented for this age group, so the long-term consequences are yet to be identified.

It's a very scary problem, and it's one of the biggest issues of our generation. In my mind, we can all help. Governments need to regulate it. Parents need to regulate it. And kids need to understand the issues around using it. Because untreated, the impact of mental health is devastating.

Looking after the wellness of society is one of the most important things we can do. Luckily, there's more help available and we're all getting better at seeking help. The stigma of seeing a psychologist or a counsellor isn't like it used to be. And that's such a great way forward for all of us.

Why now?

The wellness economy is worth trillions of dollars. And, according to the Global Wellness Institute, this figure takes in a range of segments including healthy eating, traditional and complementary medicine and personal care.

Mental wellness is a fast-growing sector of this market and, as you'll read, there's a strong financial return in improved health and productivity, so companies invest millions in the wellness economy.

INSIGHTS FROM BRYDIE HUGGINS

Brydie Huggins is an educational psychologist who specialises in mental health in children. I have known Brydie my entire life. Our families grew up together and she used to babysit us when we were kids! Brydie is one of the best child psychologists in Australia and I feel very fortunate to have her input in the book.

What's different about mental health today is that we've never had so many serious referrals, and for younger people. Interestingly, most of them are self-referrals, which is great because it means young people are much better at seeking help these days. Unfortunately, those referrals are much more serious than in the past, with a lot more risk, suicide ideation and self-harm. I am working with junior schools and have never seen as much risk, particularly with grades 5 and 6, in suicide ideation, which we haven't come across as much previously. This is very significant and we're trying to work out why this is the case, as we saw it grow before COVID-19 — though COVID-19 was the icing on the cake.

There are many factors at play here. Young people are now more educated than ever and are better at identifying their own mental health issues than many adults. They're also more willing to talk to their friends about how they're feeling than other generations. Social media is a big factor, along with other issues such as climate change and where they sit in this world, as they are exposed to so much more information than in any other generation in history. Lockdowns also had a large impact on kids, who were exposed to social media and lacking connection with family because parents or caregivers were working, as well as being physically being locked away and isolated.

The truth is that many parents have to work to support the lifestyle that they have. We see a lot of guilt with parents. They aren't there as much for their children, so they might buy things for them, or offer them more activities. But kids need more of a simple life — just being with mum and dad.

I speak to a lot of adolescents, and although many don't get to spend as much time with their parents as they would like, they almost always appreciate it when they do. For example, sitting down to dinner together is so important.

The biggest thing we saw during the lockdowns was that many families weren't available or equipped to sit down and talk about big emotions with their kids. When adolescents experience those big emotions, they adopt coping strategies that aren't great, such as self-harm and thinking about wanting to kill themselves.

Equally, adults aren't great with regard to sitting with big emotions. They don't want their children to experience disappointment, so they shelter them from emotions, and use distraction instead. In fact, experiencing disappointment as a child is a critical part of life. If you distract from emotion, it's still there only to return later.

Instead, we need to do more about accepting emotion for what it is. We need to normalise it and sit with a young person to help them through their feelings. We need them to learn that it's okay not to get their own way and that we grow by learning to accept that you can't always get what you want. They need to understand that they will be able to cope later in life. Even when children are young and they cry, this is expressing emotion. As parents, we try to make them stop crying. Crying is healthy and natural, and while it can be difficult when your child is upset, it's okay to sit with the discomfort because emotions are part of life. We don't need to push them out because they are uncomfortable. Emotions are growth and we grow from feeling them.

Key points from Brydie:

- No-one can do everything by themselves; we all need help at times.

(continued)

- If you notice that something about your life doesn't feel quite right, know that it's normal. It's okay not to be okay. The more you can talk about your emotional state, challenges and feelings, openly and honestly, the better the chance of accessing help.

- Knowledgeable people are available to help you, so ask a counsellor or psychologist about your experience.

- If you've started seeing someone for support but they don't entirely give you what you need, or you don't 'click' with them, it's okay. Go to someone else. Therapists have strengths and weaknesses and many different areas of specialty, and all psychologists, psychiatrists, counsellors and other support services are different. Look for someone who understands you and knows how to help your specific situation, someone who feels right. It's okay to shop around — they're out there!

- Fortunately, there are generally lower levels of stigma associated with mental illness among young people. Young people tend to be quite good at observing their friends for changes in behaviour, and are more willing to talk to or suggest a friend talks to a teacher or therapist.

- Speak up as early as possible, to a trusted person, or call a support hotline (google 'anonymous helpline').

Move Your Mind with Brydie: Keep a mood chart

A mood chart is a great way to give your body a daily assessment to keep track of how you feel at certain points of the day. Essentially, you rate your mood from 1 to 10, where 1 is the worst and 10 is the best, every day — once in the morning and once again in the afternoon or evening. Try to record your numbers on a chart at the same time each day, and you can also add in comments about other things that pop up during the day, such as your sleep, pain levels, alcohol or other substance consumption, anxiety or anything else that might mean something for you. If you are taking medication, it's also helpful to note any changes in your dosage or products.

I believe the key way to effect global change in mental health is to go back to school. We need to look at the effects of mental health on children and create more sustainable solutions.

If we can educate children to learn about these issues from a young age, it'll go a long way to preventing some of the mental health issues that may come along later down the track.

I know without a doubt that having some sort of education or awareness would have gone a long way in helping me as I grew up, and I know I'm not alone.

But you don't have to be, and hopefully this book will go some way towards bridging the gap.

Embedding mental health education into schooling is critical. I believe it's one of the key ways we can make long-term and sustained change in the mental wellbeing of society. There has been a lot of progress in recent years, especially with some schools using tools such as mindfulness and meditation, but we have a long way to go. The best way to do this is to make emotional education as much a part of the schooling system as other core learning areas such as English and Mathematics; it should be a fundamental part of how we're raised. If we can be taught how to understand ourselves and others better from an early age—how to have better relationships, how to communicate emotions and get the help we need—we will avoid many future problems.

It's also worth noting the role of parents. A big part of this is the emotional education we receive from our parents. Often parents have been taught old-school views from their own parents and haven't received emotional education through schooling. It's passed down from generation to generation, and we need to break the pattern. By educating children from an early age, they will bring that learning home and help to re-educate parents. It will also break the pattern so that they can educate their own children to be better placed emotionally.

Key mental health conditions

Recognising problems and making change is not only good for your wellbeing, it's also good across the board. Research from one of Australia's big audit research corporates, PwC (PriceWaterhouseCoopers), shows that for every dollar spent on improving mental health in the workplace, organisations can expect to get $2.30 back. This means that companies are better off in the long run helping someone during a period of being unwell because it's more costly to hire and train someone new.

One of the most common mental health issues and conditions is depression.

According to the WHO,

Depression is a common mental disorder affecting more than 264 million people worldwide. It's characterised by persistent sadness and a lack of interest or pleasure in previously rewarding or enjoyable activities. It can also disturb sleep and appetite; tiredness and poor concentration are common.

As we know, depression is a huge issue right now. Its effects can be long-lasting, recurrent and they can severely affect a person's ability to lead a happy and rewarding life. There are many causes of depression, including social, psychological and biological factors, with one commonality: depression doesn't discriminate. While life events can certainly lead to depression, the condition can affect anyone, regardless of how much money you make, how much you have achieved or where you come from. It affects all types—young, old, rich and poor—without discrimination.

The impact of depression is far reaching. While psychological and pharmacological treatments exist for moderate and severe depression, its effects and associated mental disorders can have a profound impact on everything—from physical health to schooling, work, and relationships with family and friends.

Depression is incredibly complicated, and we need more education to understand it and how to deal with it. Despite there being more global awareness than ever before, we still have a long way to go to de-stigmatise mental health and many other mental health disorders, including OCD (Obsessive Compulsive Disorder) and bipolar disorder.

These conditions are no different from any physical condition people may have. Some people have problems with their joints, some people are allergic to certain foods and some people have mental health disorders. All are manageable, and none are a reflection on the individual. We need to educate people more about this so they don't feel so alienated when dealing with them. Many people do not talk about their mental health disorders at work for fear of losing their job or being judged. This must change. Would someone with a broken leg feel like they need to hide it from their boss for fear of getting fired?

Let's look at some examples and descriptions of different mental health disorders.

Mood disorders

This could be anything from depression to bipolar disorder. Bipolar disorder causes extreme mood changes that affect or disrupt daily life.

Anxiety disorders

Anxiety disorders are some of the most common disorders and they can be treated. Everyone experiences a bit of anxiety, but once it becomes debilitating, it needs to be treated. The good news is that it's very treatable. People with chronic anxiety will often experience irrational fears and obsessive thoughts that won't go away. OCD is an example of an anxiety disorder involving having unreasonable and unwanted thoughts and fears that lead to compulsive behaviour.

Obsessive compulsive disorder (OCD)

Tom Corboy is a licensed psychotherapist and executive director of the OCD Center of Los Angeles who says that someone with OCD doesn't just have random thoughts, but more repeated thoughts that cause great distress because they are incongruent with how a person thinks of themselves. As someone with OCD issues, I consider this a really accurate description, and it might ring true for you or someone you know.

Personality disorders

Personality disorder refers to a long-term pattern of thinking, behaviour and emotion that is extreme and inflexible. It causes distress and makes it hard to function in everyday life.

Eating disorders

Eating disorders involve an unhealthy relationship with food, such as anorexia or bulimia. Anyone can develop an eating disorder, and we talk more about this in chapter 6.

Trauma-related disorders

An example of a trauma-related disorder is PTSD (Post Traumatic Stress Disorder), where a mental health condition is triggered by a terrifying event. The symptoms can include flashbacks, nightmares, severe anxiety and uncontrollable thoughts about the event, resulting in difficulty adjusting and coping with daily life.

Substance abuse disorders

These involve addictions such as drugs and alcohol, which often develop as a coping mechanism for a bigger problem. They can be treated provided the individual is willing to put in the work to make a change.

Developmental disorders

Examples of developmental disorders include ADHD, learning disabilities such as dyslexia, Asperger's syndrome and autism. There's a lot of stigma around disorders such as autism that needs to be removed. Autism mainly affects communication and behaviour.

Burnout/overwhelm

Burnout and overwhelm are two of the biggest problems facing the modern world. It's incredibly difficult to switch off from work when you're connected 24/7, and burnout results when you're emotionally, physically and mentally exhausted. Prolonged stress is often the main cause, making it increasingly difficult to meet constant demands.

The effects of burnout include reduced productivity and less energy, leaving you feeling helpless, hopeless, cynical and resentful. Eventually, you may feel like you have nothing more to give.

This starts to spill over into other areas of your life, including your home, work and social life. And it can cause serious, long-term changes to your body that make you vulnerable to illnesses like colds and flu.

We all have bad days, but it's a sign you could be burned out if simple things like getting out of bed and completing basic tasks become overwhelming. This usually happens over time and is most often linked to work-related issues, but can also occur from any number of situations, such as a breakup, losing a loved one or feeling a lack of purpose.

Sometimes it can be hard to catch the early signs in someone you know, or in yourself, of the risk of a mental health issue developing, and of potential burnout. Here are some signs to look out for that you might recognise:

- constant self-doubt

- feeling like an imposter

- feeling like a failure

- feeling trapped

- no motivation

- feeling lost

- not enjoying anything

- hiding away from responsibilities

- feeling tired all the time

- getting sick regularly

- headaches

- loss of appetite

- isolating yourself

- using drugs, food or other things to cope (addiction)

- erratic behaviour

- increased consumption of alcohol, cigarettes, caffeine, etc.

- difficulty concentrating

- increased errors at work

- conflict with friends, family or team members at work

- difficulty sleeping

- weight loss or weight gain

- unkempt appearance

- slower reaction times

- loss of temper.

Failure and rejection

It's hard not to get upset when things don't go your way. According to a 2012 article in *Psychology Today* titled 'Connect to Thrive', stress due to conflict in relationships leads to increased inflammation levels in the body. Physically and psychologically, we experience social connection as positive and rejection or loneliness as negative. That 'sting' of rejection turns out to be a real thing.

I reframe this by looking at the situation a bit differently.

Whenever you put yourself out there, go on a date, a job interview or try to achieve a major goal, instead of looking at it as 'failing' or 'winning', reframe it into 'I will achieve the goal' or 'I will learn something'.

If you look at life this way, then there's no 'failing', but rather a chance to grow. We learn just as much when things don't go our own way (often more) than we learn when things do, so by trying as many things as possible, you'll always be learning.

Whenever you feel uneasy, nervous, doubt yourself or feel like backing out of a confronting challenge, remind yourself of this, and reframe your mind to accept failure as simply a chance to grow. You'll read more about this later in the book.

Suicide

You read earlier that one person commits suicide every 40 seconds. I framed my TEDx talk around this statistic, concluding as I had finished my presentation that more than 27 people had taken their lives during the 18-minute delivery, according to the figures. It's horrific.

One of the key points in my talk is something I find particularly remarkable: the number of people who attempt suicide by jumping off the Golden Gate Bridge in San Francisco. Sadly, jumping off the iconic bridge is also a common way to end one's life. Of the thousands of people who have jumped off the Golden Gate Bridge, only about thirty-five have survived.

Every single survivor, comprising men and woman at the lowest ebb of their lives, said exactly the same thing when interviewed. They all said that the second they jumped, they regretted it instantly.

Think about that for a second. If of the about thirty-five people known to have survived a suicide attempt on the Golden Gate Bridge had the same experience, it's a safe bet to assume that the thousands who didn't survive thought the same thing.

One of those survivors is a man named Kevin Hines. Kevin attempted suicide by jumping off the bridge in 2000 and survived. He has since become an activist, dedicating his life to travelling around the United States, and the world, spreading positive messages around dealing with mental health related issues.

These days I'm very fortunate to spend a large portion of my life speaking to thousands of kids and adults about mental health. And what never ceases to amaze me is how many people out there are hurting. The stories I hear day in and day out are so alarming; it seems like every person I speak to has been touched by suicide in some way. It's affected a friend, a friend of a friend, a loved one, a colleague … it goes on and on.

If you look at the statistics, it's not surprising:

- An estimated 1 million people die from suicide worldwide each year.

- Issues such as clinical depression, bullying, body shaming, social isolation, substance abuse and severe physical disease are factors that can lead to suicide.

- Globally, the suicide rate for men is twice as high as for women.

- Suicide is the leading cause of death in Australia for people aged between 15 and 44 years of age.

Why is this happening?

People commit suicide over various situations: bullying, relationship issues, feeling helpless, financial problems and loneliness, self-hatred and, these days, social media–related issues — and not just from cyber bullying. Kids are killing themselves as they compare themselves to false realities projected on social media—they are comparing the dullest parts of their lives to a manufactured highlight reel and are asking, 'Why am I not enough?'

Something I come across often is a common theme: bottling up emotions and believing there's no way out. This is a false narrative that we feed ourselves as the truth. If there is one thing I want to get across—and one thing only—it's that there is *always* an answer and help is *always* out there. No matter how bad you feel, no matter how long your false narrative has been feeding you, there's *always* a solution other than suicide.

Personally, I've never been at a point of considering suicide. Having said that, I have many times been at the point of losing hope, feeling completely and utterly numb to the point of not remembering what it felt like to feel anything, and seeing no way out. It's a hopeless and terrifying experience and a feeling I wouldn't wish on my worst enemy.

I've been fortunate that I've always been a dreamer and no matter how bad things have gotten for me mentally, I've convinced myself that they will someday get better. And they always do, with hope being the only thing that got me through those periods.

Importantly, these experiences have taught me to understand just how bad it must be for people who get to the point of attempting suicide. If I felt that horrible, then how much mental turmoil must they be in? My own suffering has given me the gift of empathy. Empathy for anyone else suffering, and a shared knowledge that we can all beat this.

The other gift it has given me is learning that we really can get through anything. No matter how helpless we feel, and how overwhelming a situation may be, if we just hang in there, things will change. A lot of things in life are unfair, unplanned and uncertain, but if we learn to hang on and reach out for help, we can overcome anything.

It scares me to think that I could easily have been one of these people had I not asked for help. If I hadn't learned to seek out the support of my family, friends and sometimes professionals, I can honestly say that I may not be here today. So, please speak up because there's no weakness in admitting you have a problem. Instead, there's strength in vulnerability.

From what I've learned, when it comes to vulnerability, the more love and care that we decide to put out into the world, the more likely it is we will heal ourselves. When we stop looking at what we can personally take out of each situation and start acting selflessly we will find ourselves with more joy and love in our lives than we could have previously imagined.

Always put your mental health first

Many of us make the mistake of putting other people's issues above our own. While I believe you should make an effort to help as many people as you can, often we get so caught up helping others that we forget to look after ourselves. This is not sustainable and can often lead to burnout, preventing us from being able to give sound advice. If you put yourself first, you'll be much clearer, calmer and able to help people in the right way.

Here are some tips for putting yourself first:

- Never forget to look after yourself.

- Don't let your health decline because you're looking after someone else.

- Know your limits and only take on what you can.

- Have a support team around you.

- Always get outside help when you need it.

- Always check in with yourself while helping others.

INSIGHTS FROM DR RICHARD CHAMBERS

Dr Richard Chambers is a clinical psychologist and leading mindfulness expert. I collaborated on a project with Richard several years ago and have stayed in touch since. I love his authenticity and quality of work, and I'm very lucky to be able to share his insights here and elsewhere in the book.

My work these days is largely about helping people get back into their bodies in line with the big trend of connection and disconnection. The body is always providing an abundance of information, and whether things are in balance or out of balance, life gets really fascinating when you start paying attention to yourself.

So, in my work I help people really start to listen to themselves and feel emotion, using exercise as the catalyst for change. Right now, this represents the biggest pattern of what I'm seeing — people not being connected with their bodies and, as a result, disconnecting and burning out. For example, the typical presentation in my practice is successful, high-functioning entrepreneurs with relationship or major health problems.

I'm no different, really, as this has been my history too. I was so driven and busy that I wasn't really listening to myself, which led to some adrenal fatigue. While I began to feel run down and burned out, on the flipside, everything else in my life was great. I thought, 'If my life feels so aligned with the work I am doing, and it is meaningful beyond the person and helping humanity, then how can I possibly be burning out?' It was only when I looked deep inside myself and saw my core, this little bit of ego, that I got my answer. To be honest, it was insecurity and overcompensation where I would push myself, and that's been the source of a lot of my problems in my life. By acknowledging this, I got myself back into my body, and now I help my clients get back into their bodies too.

Starting to exercise more means that you can progress quicker, because you can really start feeling your body and being more connected with your emotions. From the moment you start listening to your body, you're not lost in your head. Instead, you start focusing on your body's physical needs, and suddenly you're not so anxious or depressed because you start to then reconnect with your emotions. As you start meeting your own physical, emotional and relational needs better, you're more present with yourself and others, which helps mental health problems subside. A different way to look at this is to imagine that people who are deeply connected are like trees with their roots deep in the earth and their leaves ready for the sun. If a big storm rolls in, the tree remains cool and flexible because it's deeply rooted in the earth. If you don't have that kind of connection, you can get blown away more easily.

Creating meaningful values is interesting too. Not only does exercise have cardiovascular benefits, but it also provides clarity about what's important in your life. What do you want to contribute to the world? What do you want your life to be about? My definition of value is what you actually give your time and attention to. For example, I ask people, 'What do you value in life?' They might answer, 'Connection and family'. Then I'll ask, 'Great, but what do you actually give your attention to?' And they'll say 'Work, success, distractions on my phone'. They're not aligned, and this is a great example of how people are disconnected with themselves. Try it yourself — it can be a bit of a bombshell moment.

Day-to-day, my key theme for you is to reconnect. Exercise, meditate and start to feel your body work daily. Don't put your headphones on, go for a run outside in a park along a river; be outside with the trees, birds and silence, and just enjoy the natural world. Adding to this, get good sleep, eat an anti-inflammatory diet, and truly connect with your partner. Ensure

(continued)

you have face-to-face human connections with people who matter, not just random people. If you're connected with people, connected with the natural world and connected with a hope for a future, meaningful values and work, that's a fantastic source of genuine resilience. These are all things that make a massive difference in my life and I'm constantly coaching people that making these changes will help them become healthier, more resilient and happier.

My message is that you must make all these important things a priority. We have just experienced a global pandemic, which disconnected us and forced us into periods of isolation. Mental health problems started presenting and so we realised that face-to-face connections are important, which has been a massive blessing. We also moved more relationships online, onto social media and Zoom, which has taken away the opportunity for actual face-to-face human contact. We've realised that it's not enough, and suddenly it really shook us. Now, we realise the need for human interaction, especially with those closest to us.

My work in mental health

Over the past decade, I've been fortunate to deliver thousands of mental health seminars around Australia and internationally. I've spoken in a mix of environments ranging from primary and secondary schools, large corporates, suburban factories and sporting clubs to remote villages in India, to name a few. The number of people I've been fortunate to meet, the stories shared and the vulnerabilities I've witnessed have been some of the biggest gifts I've received.

What stands out to me time and time again, and what I've learned most over 10 years, is the universal power of vulnerability and storytelling. From day one of speaking about my own mental health battle in schools, I simply shared my own personal story. I stood up and spoke from the heart, making a point not to sugar-coat anything; just to be raw, real and honest. A decade later, the core of what I do remains the same, and I can see the way people sit up and take notice when I begin to talk about the struggles of my personal life.

There have been so many stories from the past 10 years of talks. People approach me afterwards or in a break and feel compelled to share. I really enjoy simply listening, taking in everything they wish to tell me and being present with them.

From that, I've seen how everyone, despite their political views, upbringing or situation, just wants to be heard and hear from others. By being vulnerable and talking about emotional obstacles, we let people know that they are not alone and that their problems are universal. Suffering is part of the human condition and life will always have ups and downs, but often we tell ourselves that we are unique in our problems, that no-one else is as weak as we are and that we are pathetic for not coping. This could not be further from the truth.

Absolutely everyone struggles in different ways and we all just want to be heard. Humans can handle adversity, but what will break us is losing hope. And we gain hope from hearing about similar struggles to our own. This is the power of vulnerability and storytelling.

It's something I hope you keep in mind when reading the selected stories below. I hope they inspire you to do more sharing yourself, not just to help yourself but also to improve the lives of others.

Cutting through corporates

I have hosted several talks and workshops in corporate environments, some with executives in large organisations. On one occasion I was leading a high-level workshop with the CEO and other key executives of a multibillion-dollar company. They clearly did not want to be there and were very dismissive in their body language when we started. It was clear that they felt that sitting around and talking about their emotions was taking them away from valuable productivity and money-making time.

It's fair enough to feel that way since, regardless of your occupation, there are tasks that must be completed each day to progress your career and pursuits. But among this constant moving forward, we often forget to take a moment to breathe, check in with our emotional needs and make time to connect.

I could feel the tension in the room. After I was asked several condescending questions, I decided to change tack and revert to what always works—vulnerability. I disarmed them by talking about my own shortcomings, my nervousness and feelings about their hostility, and explained that I understood why they wouldn't want to be in a room wasting time talking about mental wellbeing.

I then shared my own story and tried my best to adapt my approach on the spot to cut through to their viewpoints. It worked. Shortly after sharing this, I challenged them to share their own stories of overcoming adversity. I knew they were used to being pushed and put under pressure so I framed it that way, asking who would be willing to share first.

After a minute of complete silence, the CEO put up his hand. I couldn't believe it because he was known in the organisation as being especially guarded and unemotional. But he began to talk. He struggled in the beginning, but to his credit, pushed himself to keep going, sharing a very personal family matter that he had not even talked about with his closest friends. It was a beautiful thing to see him open up like that for the first time and once he got going, he couldn't stop. By the end, he was in tears, as were many of us in the room, and one by one, these emotionally guarded executives started sharing very personal matters.

The session went well over time and we could have kept going all night. You could see and feel the relief and joy in that room as they were quickly learning that it's okay to be open and honest and that people wouldn't judge or treat them differently for doing so. Following the session, the CEO went from sharing his own story in that room for the first time to putting his hand up to speak regularly within the company, attending my other talks and sharing his story to encourage others, and even filming his story to share with the broader company. You could visibly see the child-like enthusiasm in his body language. He was like a kid again wanting to help others, putting his ego aside and reconnecting with what it feels like to be in touch with emotions and to be able to help those around him. He has now had a lasting impact in that company.

Bottling up emotions

I'd been running seminars for a large group in a big, suburban manufacturing company. We finished for the week on one Friday afternoon, after a session had gone very well. As we were packing up, I was approached by one of the workers. He was a leader in the group, and someone everybody looked up to — always a voice of reason both at work and at home. He was the type of person who was always looking after and helping others.

He quietly came up to me and asked to talk. He was hesitant at first but explained that after hearing me share my story and talk about vulnerability, now was the time to share his. He explained that he had had an active plan to end his life that coming weekend. He had meticulously planned it, tying up his affairs and making sure his wife and kids were looked after with a plan in place.

As he was explaining this, he started to realise the gravity of what he was planning to do. He'd reached this point after 30-plus years of bottling up every emotion that tried to come to the surface. But he was finally at boiling point.

By speaking about it so openly he was able to see there were other options and I could see the enormous relief on his face. Following our talk, he started working with a psychologist and the company's human resources team to work through his issues. He had some time off before returning, not only to talk openly with his family, but also to speak out to his entire team at work, sharing what he had been through and using his story to help others. He is now vocal about suicide prevention and continues to inspire and help others in the workplace to manage their own issues.

It was incredible to see someone move from being suicidal with an active plan, to confronting it and creating an environment and tools to deal with it, and then going on to help others overcome their own obstacles.

Seeking help can be life saving

A few years ago, I was due to fly out to a site belonging to a national company in Australia as part of a speaking tour when the session was suddenly put on hold because an employee had taken his own life on site.

I later learned that he had a loving family and had never shown any signs of mental illness.

However, he left behind a notebook in which he detailed how he had been bullied by a colleague over many years. He wrote that he had felt trapped and didn't know how to cope, putting on a brave face for decades. Eventually, he could no longer deal with the shame but, sadly, instead of seeking help, he took his life.

Following an investigation, it was found that the bully had severe mental issues of his own. I couldn't help thinking: could this have been prevented if they had scheduled my session before that fatal day or if the employee had accessed education and information on mental health? It's a lesson in how important it is to look after ourselves and others every chance we can.

Getting in early

I started out my career in mental health speaking at schools — and I still do. Being able to go into schools and connect with teenagers by sharing my own story in their situation has been one of the greatest experiences of my life.

Often, it's the first time these kids have been given a chance to connect in this area and to have an opening to talk about their own issues. So, I always try to be as raw and relatable as I can. During and after the sessions, countless kids build the confidence to speak out about their issues. They often tell me that they find it hard to relate to hearing clinical information from someone two to three times their age. They want to be heard and hear something they can translate into their own lives. As a result, the number of kids I have met and the stories I have heard have been amazing.

Not that long ago, I was speaking at a school and sharing my story. Afterwards, the school captain asked his teacher if he could sit privately and talk with me. He was a true leader in the school, dominating in every sporting event, with top grades, and had every girl in the school chasing him. But underneath that he felt enormous pressure. His family had huge expectations of him and he wasn't enjoying the many sporting and academic pressures that lay ahead. He just wanted to make mistakes and enjoy being a teenager. We sat down and he opened up to me about all of this. It was the first time he had spoken to anyone, and he burst out crying.

Afterwards, he explained how much of a relief it was speaking about it and decided to make some changes. He spoke to his family and the school and opened up about the situation. I checked in with him months later and he was receiving professional help, was closer with his family than ever and was finally happy at school. It was such a nice thing to hear. It's important that the education system caters to mental wellbeing and, as I discussed, I feel very strongly about embedding systems in the future to ensure we can provide the tools that kids so desperately need to thrive in life.

A bit about stress

According to a Headspace article titled 'How to Relieve Stress', when you're stressed, various things happen in your brain. The area of the brain involved in emotional processing, the amygdala, sends a distress signal to the hypothalamus. This then kickstarts the 'fight or flight' response — which you've probably heard of — and initiates stress hormones (including adrenaline) to flood your body. Your heart beat increases, you breathe more heavily and your body sends additional oxygen to your brain. But if you keep activating this response, your body can suffer health problems such as high blood pressure. It's really important to manage the way your body deals with stress. Headspace suggests trying these great stress-busting activities:

- *Go for a 10-minute stroll.* Take a walk to relax your mind and clear your head. Using big muscle groups repetitively helps to reduce stress, and even 10 minutes is enough. It can help you sleep better too.

- *Listen to music.* Did you know that listening to music can change your heart beat? Our heart starts to sync in time to the musical beat, so a gentle song can help to reduce a racing heart beat.

- *Start talking.* Vent, share and complain. Research shows that this is really good for your mental health. Calling friends is equally valid, or failing that, talking to a therapist can help you relieve stress in your body and mind.

A final word

In my lifetime, I've seen more psychologists than I can recall. And while extremely beneficial, the process can also be exhausting and expensive. The government's support and rebates are not enough for regular psychology — nor are they sufficiently practical — and if you're one of the lucky few who can afford to see a psychologist weekly, it's often nowhere near enough to get on top of the problem at hand.

It goes back to the analogy about exercise: if you hired the best personal trainer to talk to about a fitness regime for one hour per week, would that alone be enough to get you in shape? Possibly not. Understanding mental health is not enough. Seeing a psychologist is only one piece of the puzzle. You need to be doing small daily things, all of which I explain in part III. And if you need essential medication, consult with a doctor or a psychiatrist and trial the best options for you under supervision rather than seeing trigger-happy doctors telling you to try a certain medication without a second thought. Some days are easy and many others are hard; it's a daily grind but one more valuable than anything else I have ever encountered.

Move Your Mind with Nick:
My three go-to tools

To kick things off, I'd like to share with you the three actions that have seen me through many hard times.

They are a simple go-to for when you're starting to struggle. There's no checklist of 20 things to do—just three tools that will give you some guidance. Each of these will be detailed throughout the book, and together they create a powerful course of action.

1. *Seek help.* I always say that the one thing you should never do is nothing. When you're struggling, it's important you take that first step. It could be calling a friend, speaking to someone at work, or, if you don't know where to begin, simply going to Google and typing in 'free mental health helpline'. This will lead to an anonymous conversation to help you get onto the process of getting the help you need.

2. *Change your routine.* The next step is around changing your routine and creating new habits. Habits are such a big part of creating positive mental health, and you'll read much more about this throughout the book.

3. *Build a team around yourself.* No-one can do everything on their own, so having a team is essential to success. Build a team and remind yourself that none of us can do it alone.

MY THREE GO-TO TOOLS

At one point or another, we've all faced a problem that felt so big it seemed impossible to solve. When you're facing an overwhelming challenge, it's easy to freeze up and forget what you're supposed to do to make positive progress.

If you need help, if you want to make a change or if you are not sure where to go for support, this Three Things First tool will help you to break out of your panicked state and start moving toward success once more.

Take that first step!!!

Seek help

Change your routine and practise a new habit for 21 days or more.

Build a team around yourself.

Tap into these three things for what to do when you do not know where to go, or how to begin.

PART II
HEALING AND SHARING

In part II, we look at how to own your mental health story. No two stories are identical, so only you can work through yours to begin the healing journey. But you're not alone. Chapter 3 is packed with tips and tools as well as other people's personal stories—all of which will help you along the way.

An important part of healing is talking about your journey without shame. People learn through sharing stories and we grow through conversation. Both lead to vulnerability and vulnerability leads to healing. Sometimes all we need is to hear from someone going through a similar battle to ours to remind us that we're not alone. If we all start sharing stories and having conversations, collectively we can change the world.

A LOT OF PEOPLE THINK CELEBRITIES ARE IMMUNE TO MENTAL HEALTH, BUT THE TRUTH IS CREATIVE PEOPLE PROBABLY SUFFER MORE AND WE SEE IT ALL THE TIME WITH OVERDOSES AND SUICIDES.

Sarah Jeffery

CHAPTER 3
OWN YOUR STORY

After reading part I, you should have a good understanding of mental health and you may be able to recognise some signs of risk. It's now time to take the first practical step on your journey to better health. This involves owning up to yourself and being vulnerable as you confront some difficult home truths. The very first step is to own your narrative—your story.

Why should I own it?

To own your story is to acknowledge the truth of your experience, without shame, and to support your personal wellbeing through conversation and self-observation.

Basically, it's your first step towards becoming well and healthy. It's the ability to talk candidly about your journey, the different things you suffer from, how you've identified them and the things you can do to heal.

We all have our own stories made up of our different experiences—both learned and innate. And while your own story is yours alone, there will always be someone going through a similar battle. We often feel like our struggles are unique to us, when the reality is many people are going through similar battles. Some things are harder to deal with than others, but by sharing stories and experiences we can help each other to understand that it's okay, it's part of life and we can get through it.

When you can't control everything, the rollercoaster of life can often leave you with overwhelm, extreme stress and burnout. There's also a strong element of shame when it comes to owning your story. When you feel ashamed of your suffering, it adds to a feeling of isolation. When you're unhappy or unfulfilled in some way, it can make you feel disconnected from everyone else.

This, coupled with the continuing stigma around mental health, can make it even harder to reach out. When everyone is pretending they're fine but under the surface they're not, the stigma is perpetuated, which adds to the overall epidemic.

That's why it's important to stop the cycle and develop the confidence to own your own mental health story.

It only takes one person

It can take just one person to speak out about their story—whether it's someone high profile like a singer, actor or celebrity, or someone closer to home in your family or school—to start the conversation that you may need to have regularly.

You may recall the story in part I about the factory worker who had planned to end his life the next day but after attending my talk, thankfully changed his mind. Had he not been part of the session, he may not be with us today.

Luckily, I was able to guide him to the right resources as well as help him find the professionals he needed for rehabilitation. He couldn't believe he was feeling so ashamed and worried, but he worked through his rehabilitation and was able to head back to work.

Now passionate about sharing his experience, he's a fantastic success story all because he began owning his story.

INSIGHTS FROM SARAH JEFFERY

Sarah Jeffery is a Canadian-American actress, singer and dancer best known from the NBC series Shades of Blue, *Disney Channel's* Descendants *and The CW Network's* Charmed. *I met Sarah as we shared the same acting agency in Vancouver. She has had a lot of success in her film and TV career and uses her profile to spread positive messages about mental health and other issues close to her heart. She shared her story on my podcast and was kind enough to do the same here. I felt it was a story that had to be shared because it has the power to help a lot of people.*

From the time I came into the world, I felt anxious. As a baby, I wouldn't sleep, I cried all the time and so I feel like it wasn't really a shock to my parents that I began to experience more severe anxiety and other symptoms. I think I was around seven or eight when I had my first real stroke of panic attacks and heavy-duty anxiety, which happened while I was on a ferry boat. We were caught up in a horrible storm and it was really scary, with fires on board, broken windows and stuff. I had a fear of the wind and I think it was like a trigger point for all the anxiety that had manifested in my life so far. It was kind of like opening Pandora's box.

From then on, I really, really struggled. First, it was just a fear of the wind, and now, looking back, I can see there were some

(continued)

definite OCD tendencies. I used to constantly check outside over and over again and now I look back and I feel for that kid. My parents had no idea, and I had no idea what was going on either. All I knew was that I was in this emotional turmoil all the time.

Then I hit puberty and things started to really hit the rails again. I was in Grade 8 or 9 when, again, I had my first strokes of the kind of OCD I suffer with now. Intrusive thoughts all the time, repetitive behaviours and something else called Harm OCD.

I first started experiencing Harm OCD at around age 12. I distinctly remember one Christmas lying in bed waiting for it to be morning, and having the thought, 'What if I hurt my family?' I thought I'd be able to shake it off like any thought, but it stuck, and it grew in size, evolving to images of hurting my family or myself involuntarily. I was terrified I would sleepwalk and do something horrible, so I stayed up all night. It was one of the worst Christmases I have had; I was convinced I was a crazed killer. I didn't tell anyone anything then, out of fear that they would be as scared of me as I was of myself.

My OCD tends to make me perform incessant compulsions on a daily basis, but they're not the typical visual ones people might expect (such as turning the lights on and off or opening and closing a door). My compulsions are mostly mental. I think about a potential scenario for hours and hours, never arriving at a conclusion and feeling like if I don't figure it out, something horrible will happen. I mentally 'check' that I still love my family and my boyfriend, and if I don't like the results I will keep checking until I do, which provides only temporary relief. I then start the cycle again soon after.

My intrusive thoughts range from, 'What if I forget how to act?', to 'What if I hurt someone I love?', to mental images of disturbing violence and unwanted sexual images. They're always unwanted and, depending on the day, can prevent me from carrying on with my life.

I believed there was something wrong with me, but it was very hard to talk about until I got to a point where I just didn't think

I could go on any longer the way I was. I'm not sure exactly how it happened but my mother could see it was basically tearing me apart.

When I got my diagnosis I had no idea that OCD could be what I was struggling with. I thought OCD was about being neat and tidy and counting and everything, which was definitely a part of it, but I would call mine a more abstract version of OCD. Being diagnosed, there was a huge sense of relief that I wasn't alone and that there was a name for what I was going through, and that these thoughts were just that — thoughts — that do not define me as a person. At this time, I began therapy treatment and was prescribed an SSRI (Selective Serotonin Reuptake Inhibitor) — an antidepressant — which truly changed my life.

While I still really struggle, I can't believe how far I've come now. Truly, therapy and antidepressants changed my life and I'm really open about that. Obviously, there's a negative stigma around taking medication and people are scared it's going to change who they are, but I don't know if I would even be here without it. I really condone it if it's something you need to function. As for me, there's a chemical imbalance in my brain so I'm just balancing the chemicals so that I can function. Therapy has also been massively helpful, and I've been with my therapist for three or four years. She understands me; it's really life-changing. I'm also very blessed that I can afford therapy because I know some people can't. Support is really important.

Today, I'm an advocate for mental illness and I'm very open about my OCD, depression and anxiety. As much as I can, I try to educate people to use the term OCD properly, and to encourage them to look more into it because it's really misunderstood. Many people have the tendency to say, 'I'm so OCD', and I say to them, 'Would you say that you're so diabetes or so cancer?' Of course you wouldn't because it's offensive and rude. Using OCD in context is huge, which goes back to education and painting a

(continued)

bigger, clearer picture about what it is, along with its sub-genres and sub-categories.

I do the best I can to keep it real and am very vocal about what I'm going through. As a result, I've had tonnes of different responses, with some people who think this stuff should be kept private. But I'm focusing on what I can do for people, not people living these shiny, tidy lives and just showing a highlight reel of what's going on—it can be misleading. For people who have OCD, it's not something to be ashamed about. Even if talking about it helps just one person—whether they have it too and feel like they're not alone—or if it's someone who rethinks the way they use the term OCD.

I think there has been a lot more conversation and openness and compassion towards mental health. A lot of people think celebrities are immune to mental illness, but the truth is creative people probably suffer more and we see it all the time with overdoses and suicides. If you're struggling, I think finding a support system is really key. If you can afford to make the jump and do therapy even though it's scary, I highly recommend it. Have an open mind towards tools that can help you, even if that's an SSRI or other medication. Whatever it is, there are some really great tools out there that can help you navigate whatever you're going through.

How do you own your story?

As I've said, I acknowledge that owning your story isn't easy. It's uncomfortable and unsettling, and it involves looking at your own life, perhaps in a way you've never done before.

You might think the various people featured in this book make it look easy to own their stories because they're confident about speaking publicly, but let me refer you back to my story.

I'm the kid who used to physically vomit before having to deliver a talk to just five peers. I'm the kid who got escorted off a football oval because he grabbed a bit of grass that Gary Ablett Senior had touched. I'm the kid who hid bricks under his bed to use as weights. I'm the kid who abused alcohol, nearly killed his best friend and developed an eating disorder, about which I've never shared until now.

I can talk about all of these things now, but only because it's taken a huge amount of time, healing and rehabilitation to face my demons and get the help I've needed. You'll be reading examples of this all the way through this book, and hopefully it will help you to see that I'm right there with you because I've been through it. And you can get through it too. Just take your time, work to a schedule or at your own pace and remember to keep having a go!

Key learnings

Here are some ways to own your story:

1. *Ask for help.* Don't pretend everything is fine when you know you're struggling. The worst thing you can do is bottle it up and bear the pain all by yourself. Again, *ask for help.*

2. *Create your support network.* Draw on friends, family, colleagues and professional mental health services. Aim to have at least two to three special people in your life who you know you can call in an emergency.

3. *Contact professional health services.* If you don't have someone personal to reach out to, I recommend 24/7 services such as Lifeline, Beyond Blue or Kids Helpline in Australia and the World Federation for Mental Health,

(continued)

WHO, NAMI and the Mayo clinic in the United States. Depending on what country you are in, there will be different mental health support services. If you type 'free mental health helpline' into Google, options will come up.

4. *Develop self-awareness.* Learn to observe your thoughts without investing in them. Remember that not every image produced in your mind is accurate or helpful. Listen calmly to your thoughts before you act, and this will give you the power to pick out what's actually useful versus what's potentially harmful.

5. *Understand addiction.* Addiction isn't just about drugs or alcohol; it relates to work, relationships and food choices—the parts of life we all deal with. Addiction can camouflage itself as healthy or harmless behaviour, which can also develop into patterns of obsessive behaviour, as it did with me.

6. *Avoid sweeping problems under the carpet.* Shame and fear are overwhelming emotions that cause people to isolate themselves and hide the signs of their suffering so that they appear 'normal' to the rest of the world. The longer your illness remains untreated, the worse symptoms can become and the less likely you are to be able to access the support and treatment necessary to heal.

7. *Keep it up.* Mental health maintenance is like keeping up your physical fitness. You'll experience more consistent results if you make the maintenance tools a part of your daily routine, even when life is easy. (I'll reveal these tools in part IV.)

INSIGHTS FROM PETER CHAMBERS

I was introduced to Peter Chambers through a close friend and am privileged to have been able to interview him about how he has come to accept his terminal illness. Peter has a form of muscular dystrophy called myotonic muscular dystrophy (MMD), a disease that became personal to me after I lost my Uncle Bruce to motor neurone disease (MND). Peter is incredibly positive and inspiring and I wanted to share his story.

About 15 years ago, I was at the gym doing a cycling class and I felt numbness in one foot. I thought it was odd, so I saw a GP. Since then, I can pinpoint little snippets of symptoms over the journey. Shortness of breath and weakness in my arms and hands for three- or four-month periods, things I would never have suspected were connected to my condition. But because of the weakness, surgery was recommended. After the operation, my shoulder just fell apart instantly, and I came out of it pretty much losing the use of my right arm. I now have numbness in both feet.

After eight months of testing I was diagnosed with myotonic muscular dystrophy (MMD) in 2019. MMD is a specific form of muscular dystrophy that affects muscles and other organs in the body. I could have been diagnosed a year earlier had there been a better process in place (this may have prevented such a rapid decline), and one of the stats I learned that astounded me was that by the time you get diagnosed you've lost 70 per cent of your muscles to MMD. Clearly, things need to improve, and I'm learning as I go.

If you were talking to me five years ago, I wouldn't have inspired you. I was never one to talk. And I wouldn't have described myself as a positive person—it wasn't a natural fit for me. But

(continued)

surprisingly, the illness has really given me a mindset to speak out and help others. I've got this new life which I've sort of embraced … 'accepted' is probably a better word. The illness has given me the ability to be the best version of myself. I am the same person, but now I only focus on what's important.

I am not qualified in this area and I can't put it into neurological terms, but the way I see it is that my life now is about train tracks, and the way I am living my life is very much inside those train tracks. If I get away from the train tracks and start looking at other areas or things out of my control, I will lose focus and positivity. So, I am focused to stay on course. If I'm inside there, I'm really strong; I won't get hurt if I'm inside those train tracks. Emotionally as well as physically, I won't let little things hurt me. Occasionally, something will jump into my head and I'll wake up at 3 am and not sleep for three hours because I'm doing that thing to death. But the next day I can pull it apart and chuck out the bits that aren't relevant, recalibrate and get back into those train tracks. Just get straight back on that horse again and keep riding.

Finally, I want to discuss that there's no 'one size fits all'. My journey is completely different from the next person's, and it's always evolving. What probably helps me is that my mind is less clogged than it used to be. I've only got a handful of issues going on in my life, and they're pretty big, but if you go back five years, I had several issues going on in my head constantly. For example, in a corporate environment there are so many people you must please, and I was often bringing work home with me, trying to juggle it all. Sometimes it was great, sometimes it wasn't.

Now, it really helps me to minimise the external influences that impact my life. My life is so much simpler now than what it used to be and that's why I'm excited by the opportunities that I have now. It's the most bizarre conversation, but here we are: I've got a terminal illness and aspects of my life are better because of it. 'Fulfilling' is a good word—I've got more purpose. I think it comes back to the train tracks: to become more focused and less cluttered in your thought processes, you must get yourself in that mindset. I completely understand why people in my kind of situation struggle with things that are confronting and coming from all angles.

For me, it's simple. It's not about not having problems. It's about choosing which problems you want to focus on. You will always have things you want to deal with, so get rid of the things that are not serving you. Try to simplify, try to declutter your life.

Move Your Mind with Peter: Make it work for you

- *Use the train track analogy.* I like to put issues that are confronting me and that I have control of inside train tracks, so that I can focus on them while allowing myself to let go of other issues outside of my control. The best example I can think of is when I met my neurologist to discuss my MMD condition and I had to confront the reality that I would lose the use of my arms within the year. I used the analogy that they will become like spaghetti hanging off my shoulders and he said that's probably what it will be like. This was confronting, but because I put it in my train tracks, I knew that however bad it was, I would be able to deal with it because it was in my train tracks and I could confront it. My challenge to you is to find your own version of train tracks, place the issues that you need to face inside them and allow yourself to let go of everything outside of your control.

- *Learn to understand yourself and to know who you are.* I think I'm pretty fortunate to be able to do that and I have always had a good feeling for who I am. I think having a terminal illness has really shown me what is important and what to let go of—we can waste so much time on

(continued)

unimportant things. Really challenge yourself here and ask, 'What are my values?', 'What do I care about?', 'What could I do without?' Peel back the onion, look deep inside yourself and learn to focus on what really matters. It took a terminal illness for me to do this; I challenge you to do it too. I am happier now with a terminal illness than I ever was before and that's because I now focus on what's important. Imagine how much happier you can become!

- *Focus on the small things.* I recently had to grab a drink at a 7-Eleven with the limited use of my arms. I angled myself in and had a big smile on my face as I grabbed the drink successfully. Focus on the small things and give yourself credit for achieving them!

- *Leave a legacy.* My terminal illness has taught me the importance of my family and of leaving a lasting impact in helping people with MMD and mental health. What is more important? Always ask yourself, 'What legacy am I leaving?' Would you be proud of your legacy if you were looking back on your life? Remind yourself of this regularly and use it as fuel to do things that give you meaning, help others and make you feel happy. I now want to be a positive influence and be remembered for it. I want to help people and dedicate my final days to making as much of a positive impact as I can.

Move Your Mind with Nick:
Facing challenges

Overcoming something you fear, like facing a challenge, can lead to massive growth and personal development. It can even change your sense of self, and your life's path, for the better.

So, move your mind by choosing one thing you fear. It doesn't need to be anything big, but something that matters to you today. When you think of it, try to catch the negative thoughts as they come up. Instantly dismiss the unfavourable self-judgement and replace it with a positive, encouraging thought.

Choose it, write it down, act on it and see what happens in the process. If you're able to take control of just one issue, hopefully you'll be able to feel the power that comes from owning your own mental health.

Importantly, part of owning your story is also learning that in life there's no such thing as 'failure'—there's either gaining wisdom through your experience or getting your desired outcome. (I talk about failure in part IV.) Life rarely unfolds as you plan it, but if you can face it head-on, you're more likely to get to where you want to go—in one way or another—no matter how many unexpected obstacles you have to navigate.

Good luck!

I THINK THE ONLY WAY WE CAN CREATE CHANGE IS IF WE ARE AUTHENTIC ABOUT IT OURSELVES, AND WHAT I MEAN BY THAT IS IF WE'RE ASKING PEOPLE TO BE MORE AUTHENTIC AND MORE OPEN ABOUT MENTAL HEALTH, ARE WE ACTUALLY DOING THAT OURSELVES?

Wayne Schwass

CHAPTER 4

START THE CONVERSATION

Starting the conversation is the perfect step to follow owning your story. It sounds simple, but it's two-fold: it relates to you personally in the way you interact with people, and then it creates a ripple effect on society. Let's dig in.

Connection is a funny thing. We live in an age that's more connected than ever before. Technology can be fantastic for solving problems in modern-day life, where you can access whatever you want whenever you want, order on demand and have the information you need at your fingertips instantly.

At the same time, we're bombarded with information, often as soon as we get out of bed in the morning. We open our phone when we wake up and there are notifications, messages, emails and other distractions that lure us to stay locked on to our screens. Social media is funny and entertaining for the most part, but it actually has a more insidious, manipulative function. It's designed for people to pay continuous attention to it, with the interaction stimulating the brain's reward system and breathing life into addictive patterns of behaviour.

69

It's easy to feel helpless and unable to control the never-ending notifications — they're hard to ignore. We'll talk more about the impacts of social media later, but for now this is about how being more engaged in a screen is taking us away from what's going on in real life.

A classic example is a music concert. Back in the day, the audience would hold up their cigarette lighters and collectively sway to each song, creating an incredible light show. Now, we use mobile phones. What's worrying is that the audience films and posts the videos online, providing friends who aren't there with the experience as if they were. Being at a live performance is about exactly that: taking in the experience. Being there, being present and enjoying the action unfold in front of you, rather than being distracted and filming it to show friends afterwards.

Ironically, we're more disconnected than ever. Not only are we losing the ability to connect with others in a fun and meaningful way, like at a concert, but we're also losing the ability to listen to one another. We're not having real conversations, we've stopped connecting with people one-on-one, and we're having less human-to-human contact because we're on our devices more. All of this combines to create unhealthy behaviours, and, over time, can affect social skills and relationships, and can cause heightened levels of isolation and loneliness.

I know I fall victim to constantly checking social media, screens and news articles, using them as a distraction. I'm sure we all know the feeling when we're in social situations and the person we're talking to has their eyes glazing over, constantly checking their phone and looking around at everything other than the person in front of them. Being a better listener and not being socially disengaged is important and benefits everyone. Do you recognise this behaviour in yourself?

It may seem easier to just accept that this is how it is in the modern day. Because creating real connections is hard and takes real work.

Trying to do something as simple as 'connecting' in a world that feels so disconnected can be very challenging. You need to be able to look someone in the eye, concentrate wholly on the interaction and really listen to what they're saying.

We already know that being online so much creates bigger problems. Should we just accept that this is life nowadays? If we all have that attitude, then nothing will get better. If we all play the victim and believe there's nothing we can do about it, then everything will stay the same. Things will stay hidden, and more lives will be lost. Things left unsaid in youth will turn into bigger problems in adulthood. I'm a good example of this!

How do we change this?

We change it by taking a little step forward. You've already begun owning your story; now it's time to ask yourself a simple question: how can you make more of an effort to be more connected?

This is about limiting your usage online and instead having more meaningful interactions with people and giving back the respect they deserve. It's about starting a conversation, whether it's a bit of a chat with a neighbour or something deeper with someone about what's going on in your life. It's about bringing a new level of quality to your interactions, which will not only affect your own life, but also make a change in other people's. If we all do that, a much bigger change will happen.

We also need to learn how to talk about the tough issues. We need to start asking people critical questions such as, 'How are you going?', 'Are you okay?' and 'What's going on for you?' It may sound too confronting to have to talk to someone about, but if you don't ask, they won't tell you and it stays hidden—often with tragic consequences. The price might be the life of a loved one.

INSIGHTS FROM HUGH VAN CUYLENBURG

Hugh van Cuylenburg is the founding director of The Resilience Project. He has more than 17 years' experience in developing wellness programs with more than 1000 schools. Hugh and I have crossed paths many times over the years as we share similar trajectories in building careers as public speakers in this field. Hugh is a world leader in the area of resilience and someone I thought was important to include in this book.

A lot of people ask me, 'What do you want for your kids?' Initially, I answered, 'I want them to be happy', but then I realised what I want is for them to be able to negotiate the ups and downs of life and their way around challenges. So, I want them to be resilient!

To become more resilient, I think the most important personality traits are positivity and positive emotions. Positive emotions are so unbelievably important for resilience and outlook on life. For finding a reason to smile and laugh even when something goes wrong. For still putting yourself in situations or activities that bring joy and positive emotions, despite the challenges you might be going through. It's not a matter of not having things go wrong, it's more about being able to bounce back when something goes wrong.

For me, the conversation started as a teenager when my sister was going through mental illness with anorexia nervosa. It was really bad; she was in the hospital and it was terrifying to see the state she was in. I knew there was nothing I could do to help her, but I did have this strong feeling that I should be doing something for Mum and Dad. I wanted to make them happy again.

I had no idea what the answer was as a teenager, but I had learned that if I told stories to make the whole family laugh (I would tell ridiculous ones), then perhaps that could help. So, at that young age I learned the power of storytelling. It certainly wasn't a conscious thing — it just happened.

Fast forward 12 years, I'm living in India and I guess I asked the question I asked myself when I was a teenager: 'What is it that makes people happy? How can I bring joy to people's lives?' When I was living in India, I found the answer to this while I was living in a very poor community. Despite having no money and living in a desert village, I could feel how happy the people were with just the basics in life. I was only there for three-and-a-half months, but I felt I was the happiest I had been in my entire life. People practised gratitude, empathy and mindfulness. Now, with my work on resilience, I've realised they were cultivating positive emotions every single day in their lives, and creating amazing, authentic connections with one another. Interconnection is also a big part of resilience—knowing that when something goes wrong you have a tribe around you to help you get through it.

Sometimes, in Australia, when something does go wrong, you feel very much on your own. Research has shown that Australia has some of the loneliest people in the world; we don't feel like many people know us well and don't feel like we have many people to turn to in a crisis. Knowing that when something goes wrong you've got this tribe around you to get you through helps enormously.

I think the stronger and more authentic our connections are with the people in our lives, the better we can cope. I guess I saw the example of what it could look like back in 2008 when I was living in the village.

There's another side to building resilience, which is exercise. The more I talk to people in Australia and New Zealand who have really struggled with elements in their lives, the more I hear from them in their stories how much they managed to fight back with exercise. A lot of people will say that exercising in the morning trains your brain and rewires the way you stand in the world. You have kinder thoughts about yourself, you're proud of yourself and your achievements, and when that happens you have a kinder approach to the people around you. And you're more compassionate to the people around you because you're compassionate to yourself. I certainly feel the benefits of my exercise routine.

Key learnings

Here's how to start the conversation about mental health:

1. *Don't wait for change, create change.* Whether in an organisation, school, household or in day-to-day life, we often wait for other people to make the change. Empower yourself and become a leader in setting an example, showing vulnerability and asking people how they are. If we all make that little extra effort to look out for others, we will start to see big cultural change.

2. *Check in with yourself.* If we're not looking after ourselves, we won't be able to show up for others. Are you overwhelmed? Are you getting enough sleep, eating well, exercising, meditating and taking time out?

3. *Turn your phone off.* Take a break from screens and technology. Organise to meet up with someone you care about and either leave your phone at home or switch it off and suggest that they do the same. You will be amazed at how much of a difference it makes to have a break from technology, reconnect with yourself and others, and be fully present.

4. *Be authentic.* Show up every day and be authentic to yourself and others. Often, we expect so much from other people but don't practise what we preach. Working on yourself and becoming the best version you can will naturally lead to others being inspired to make the same change.

5. *Ask for help.* If you're suffering, never be afraid to ask for help. No-one can get through everything on their own and we all need support, no matter who we are. Talk to a friend, speak to a therapist or call an anonymous helpline. I've said it before, but I want to stress this again: the one thing you should *not* do is *nothing*. So just do something.

The first step is always daunting, but once you take it you will realise it is not as hard as it seems, and solutions will follow.

6. *Support others.* If you see someone struggling, offer support and let them know you are there for them. This can often be done by just voicing that you are here if they ever need to talk. If they're not willing to seek help, make sure you inform those close to them about your concerns, and seek professional advice if necessary.

7. *Remember that it's okay to not be okay.* This comes up a lot but can't be emphasised enough. No-one is ever okay all of the time. We all have ups and downs...it's part of the human condition. Often, we tell ourselves the story that we're the only one suffering, and ask questions such as 'Why am I so weak when everyone else can handle things?' The reality is that we're not unique and others don't handle things better. We all struggle in different ways...some people just don't voice it. The more we can speak out about our own personal struggles, and encourage others to do the same, the more we can all heal together.

8. *Practise resilience.* Resilience is about acknowledging things that are difficult and reminding yourself that they will eventually pass.

9. *Detach yourself.* We need to learn to not be attached to things. When something good happens, we should embrace it but realise it won't last forever. When something bad happens, we should acknowledge it but remind ourselves that everything, good and bad, will pass. This feeds into the learnings around resilience.

10. *Feel your emotions.* Give yourself permission to feel all of the emotions that come up in your life. Rather than pushing

(continued)

them away, ignoring them or experiencing shame for feeling certain things, embrace the emotions.

11. *Find what works for you.* Find your own version of being healthy that you can sustain on a daily basis. Look at all areas — such as sleep, diet, mental diet, exercise, meditation, relationships — and ask yourself, 'What is sustainable for me to maintain my mental health on a daily basis?'

12. *Practise connection.* No matter what situation you are in, practise connection. If you meet a stranger in a café, rather than ignoring them or making a passing comment to kill time, really listen to them and invest in the conversation. When we practise this in every daily encounter, we feel much more connected and ultimately happier in our lives.

13. *Compliment others.* Whatever situation you are in and whoever you are speaking to, there is always something positive you can say, so practise kindness. When we compliment others it makes them feel great, and in turn makes us feel great and boosts our self-esteem.

14. *Give people space.* If you sense someone is overwhelmed or needs to be left alone, don't push them. Give them space and the room to open up in their own way. This comes down to practising self-awareness in our daily lives, and making the effort to really observe others and the emotions they are feeling.

INSIGHTS FROM WAYNE SCHWASS

Wayne Schwass is a former Australian Rules football player with a distinguished career over 14 years. I have been a fan of Wayne's work for a long time. There are a lot of similarities in the work we are doing and I met him properly when he took part in one of my video programs. He has a really powerful story and simple messages and tools that anyone can use.

My experience with mental illness dates back to August 1993. I lived with multiple conditions including anxiety, depression and OCD for well over 10 years and during the final 10 years of my football career. At the time, I consciously chose to only tell four people; three were doctors and psychiatrists. I worked in the media for 12 and a half years after being diagnosed, and I finally decided to tell my family and share my story publicly, which was a liberating experience. Since then, I've been advocating for a greater awareness around mental health and trying to educate Australians with tools to stay healthy and look after their wellbeing.

I've thought about encouraging people to talk about mental health and have more conversations for a very long time. If I use my own experience, encouraging people to talk about it sounds like it's an easy thing to do. But the fact is if you're disconnected emotionally, you don't know how to think and feel, and if you don't have the vocabulary or language that allows you to communicate about what you're going through, then I believe there are a lot of people who want to talk but just don't know how to.

As a result, it can be really difficult for a lot of people who don't have the tools available or the skillset to be able to communicate what they are feeling or thinking. Many people may not even know they are on the journey yet, understand where they are

(continued)

or know how to talk about it. It's a big challenge for people, especially for those who've never spoken out before.

Then there's the stigma. While we don't feel any fear, shame or embarrassment individually talking about physical ill health, we don't have that same level of comfort surrounding mental health. There is a lot of fear, shame and guilt, so I think we have to change our attitudes and perceptions towards mental health.

I believe we do that by looking at health holistically, which means considering physical, mental and emotional health, and creating environments that invite people into those discussions where they feel safe, respected, supported and know they're not being judged. I think if we can create those environments, we can have more people prepared to begin to share their story and communicate about what's going on.

Over the past six years, I've very consciously tried to live my life according to these beliefs and expectations. I communicate and talk about my emotions and I get emotional, and I think when you do that you actually give other people around you permission to do the same. We can't tell people to talk, but what we can do is live our lives and behave in a way that gives people the opportunity to sit back and think that it could also work for them. I've seen firsthand from any number of men the willingness to step into that space, so I guess my answer is we create those conversations if we're prepared to be a part of those conversations. Because if we're not, we're not creating opportunities where people feel safe enough to come into discussions.

In terms of practical things you can do, it's important to find things that work for you because we all have our own recipes. Work on your recipe and be prepared to try things. These are the things that I work on: sleep is the most important thing that I can give myself. I have to prioritise my sleep and it needs to play an important part of my 24-hour cycle. If not, I get tired, agitated and eventually stressed, with anxiety and depression maybe coming along. So, sleep is really important. Then, there's exercise. I'm a cyclist and I'm all for moving the body. Your body benefits physiologically and from a physical health perspective, but it also reacts incredibly well from an emotional perspective due to the release of hormones. So, get out and move your body.

Then there's diet. There are four important parts of a diet: what you eat, what you consume by way of fluids, what content you consume and the fourth part, which is becoming significantly important, relationships. Are your relationships positive, constructive and supportive or are they negative, toxic and destructive? If they're negative, you need to consciously think about whether it's worth continuing those relationships because if you tolerate those types of negative relationships for too long, it impacts your mental health and emotional wellbeing. So, when I talk about diet, I'm not talking about losing weight, I'm talking about nutrition. What are you consuming? Because all of those things play a role.

I actively communicate with the key people in my network who I trust when things are going really well, but personally, I've gone through a particularly challenging 12-month period. I talk to my partner every day, I talk with my GP consistently, and I sit down and talk with my mentor, where we have some really honest conversations that are not always about work. A lot of them are about life and how I'm feeling.

The other thing I think is really important is to give yourself permission to feel your emotions — and I mean all of them. Vulnerability, insecurity, fear and the emotion of crying are very important and therapeutic. Allow yourself to think, 'What am I thinking?', 'What am I feeling?'. These are some practical ways that you can invest in your wellbeing. I think the only way we can create change is if we're authentic about it ourselves.

(continued)

Move Your Mind with Wayne: A simple exercise

This is a simple exercise I would encourage you to think about. It'll take no more than five to 10 minutes, and I challenge audiences to do it all the time when I'm engaging with them. If your wellbeing is important and you're not sure where to start, this exercise is a great starting point. You just need a pen and paper, no distractions and to answer the question as honestly as possible. There are three simple questions for those who haven't begun their wellbeing journey.

1. *Why not?* Why haven't you begun to invest in your emotions and mental health?

2. *What are the barriers?* What are you scared and fearful of, and what are those things in front of you that aren't allowing you to begin your wellbeing journey? I'll share an example: I chose not to talk because the barrier for me was fear—the fear of losing respect, losing relationships, losing opportunities and losing my career. They were the barriers that kept me paralysed from not investing in my wellbeing. When you identify or understand those things that are holding you back, you can move them out of the way or you can get rid of them, which means you then have space to invest.

3. *What can you do to start investing in your mental health?* It can be as simple as saying to yourself that you will go to bed an hour earlier every night for a week, or get up 15 minutes earlier tomorrow and go for a 10-minute walk, and sticking to it for a week.

Follow these three simple things: Why aren't I? What's holding me back? What can I do? Once you understand those and make a plan, you can start working to execute them.

Move Your Mind with Nick:
Get uncomfortable

Following on from Wayne's exercise, here are two simple activities I'd like you to try.

1. *Talk to a stranger.* Go up to someone you've never met or wouldn't normally talk to and ask them some questions. Sound terrifying? Don't look at it as something to tick off your list while reading this book, but rather see it as a chance to move out of your comfort zone. Who knows? You might even find that you enjoy it and like the freedom that opening up a dialogue with someone you don't know brings.

   The reason I'm asking you to do this is that we tend to get stuck in our set way of thinking. We surround ourselves with the same people and the same thought processes and don't give ourselves an opportunity to open our minds.

2. *Share something.* But do it with someone you wouldn't normally share with. It could be with a friend, family member or social acquaintance, and the message that I'm trying to teach you is that it's okay to be who you are. The more you are yourself, the happier you will be. And the more comfortable you become in your values and what you stand for, the less you will worry about others judging you. It's about taking the first step towards owning who you truly are.

PART III

THE FOUR PRACTICAL PATHWAYS TO MENTAL HEALTH AND WELLBEING

Once you've owned your story and started the conversation, you're ready to learn about my four pathways to better mental health: Move Your Mind, Feed Your Mind, Connect Your Mind and Still Your Mind. Each one is designed as a practical tool for you to apply to your life as you choose, and to help you create preventative behaviours using real examples, tasks and stories that show how others manage their challenges and conditions.

When it comes to our mental health and wellbeing, it's all about balance. If we don't get enough sleep we're unlikely to think clearly, won't have as much energy to exercise and will likely make poor food choices. From sleep, diet, exercise, food, mental diet, and everything in between, it is all connected. The four practical pathways are here to help you take that first step towards changing your life for the better!

And stick around for part IV of the book, where I wrap them all up for long-term continual improvement.

WHEN PERSONAL TRAINERS PUT A TELEVISION ON THE TREADMILL, IT'S ABOUT MAKING THE MEDICINE TASTE BETTER. IT'S ALSO A SAYING IN THE GYM INDUSTRY — APPLY IT TO YOUR LIFE AND FIND OUT WHAT WORKS FOR YOU THAT MAKES THE MEDICINE TASTE BETTER.

Sam Wood

CHAPTER 5

PATHWAY 1:

MOVE YOUR MIND

First up is Move Your Mind. You guessed it: this one's all about movement. Exercise is one of the most natural things you can do. Your body is built to move, and exercise keeps you healthy, both mentally and physically. Unfortunately, this has become increasingly difficult in the modern world due to the busy nature of our lives. That's because most of us spend our working lives either behind a desk or in front of a computer—or both. The impact of this sedentary lifestyle is that it leaves little time for exercise, and plenty of excuses, which I think is one of the main barriers to all healthy behaviour.

We often feel overwhelmed when seeking to incorporate exercise into our lives. The gym can be intimidating, too time consuming or too expensive, and trawling through social media looking at highlight reels of the elite few can discourage us before we step foot inside.

The key to making any change is starting small and relieving yourself of pressure. Look to create a routine that works around your schedule and that can be easily and sustainably managed, regardless of how busy you become.

In this chapter, we'll explore the importance of exercise for our mental and physical health, followed by the many benefits of exercise for mental wellbeing. We'll look at some of the science behind movement and provide expert opinions and simple tips and tools on how to use exercise as an effective preventative tool for maintaining positive mental wellbeing.

INSIGHTS FROM DR PETER LARKINS

Peter Larkins is a doctor, media personality and one of Australia's most senior specialist sports physicians. I've known Peter since I was a teenager competing in middle-distance running and started to see him after developing Achilles tendonitis. As one of the country's top sports doctors, he's also an Olympic Games middle-distance runner and someone I looked up to.

Exercise is extremely important, as evidenced many years ago and long before we placed such emphasis on mental health in society. For example, even when I started out as a young doctor in the 1970s and 1980s, we were studying depression and looking at the chemical changes that happen to people when they exercise: the so-called 'happy hormones', particularly serotonin and dopamine. Even back then, the people in the exercise groups were getting the benefit of the exercise session, and it led to them needing less medication or even a change in their medication.

As a young doctor, it was very exciting to learn that exercise is good for our mental health. Today, the physical benefits are well established and continue to evolve, with cardio exercise or strength exercise shown to be associated with improvement in heart health, diabetes and bone strength.

Traditionally, the mental and emotional benefits of exercise were probably lower on the radar, but fast forward to the last few

---

years and this is now a huge focus. Today, there is a lot more research around exercise showing a real uplift in those important neurochemical stimulators that are associated with anxiety and depression. People take antidepressants for mental health disorders, and many need to, but these chemicals can also be balanced through exercise. That's because exercise boosts endorphins, dopamine and serotonin, which are the chemicals that drugs are based on. However, you must be consistent. The science is there, but even without it we can't deny how many people rave about the benefits of exercise.

It's not just scientists saying this either. Many people say exercise is their relief. It doesn't matter if you swim, run, walk or anything in between—it's just about doing it. It's also shown that social integration, where people get out and exercise with a partner, or a friend or a mate, is ideal. You need to be selfish about making time for yourself to exercise, as it will contribute to your work life, your family, your mates and your partner more positively. An example of the important endorsement of exercise is during COVID-19, when there were four reasons to leave your house: essential shopping, work, medical care and exercise. To me, that was an acknowledgement that exercise should be an integral part of people's diet and hence the endorsement for that has been great.

Finding something that works for you is critical. You don't have to run or go to the gym and it doesn't matter if you train at 6 am or 8 pm. Evidence shows that you need just 1.5 per cent of the week committed to exercise. So, that's about 150 minutes out of 168 hours, spread out over three to four days a week. It's a small proportion compared to sleeping, eating and socialising.

The biggest reason people say they don't exercise is that they don't have time—but even the busiest people can find time. The discipline, which we all struggle with, must be brought in. If you miss one session, it's not going make a difference, but things like Pilates, group sessions and personal trainers all help people to be

(continued)

consistent and motivated to turn up. Paying money is also a big incentive! The hardest thing is starting and making the change in your lifestyle to do it. I often hear people say, 'I really struggled in the beginning', and 'I could hardly walk four laps at the oval and now I'm running 5 kilometres and I love it and I'm a new person!'

As for me, I'm someone who has always talked about blood pressure, diabetes and heart disease. But now, mental health and exercise are my strong interests and I'm a great advocate for both. I'm also a personal practitioner, having competed as a middle-distance runner in the Olympics. I know firsthand as an athlete you don't become a world champion after one training session, so often the change takes a while to evolve. The first week can be bloody hell for some people, as all sorts of obstacles can pop up. But once you start seeing the mental and physical health benefits, you really start to enjoy it. I love hearing stories from people who have lost 30 kilograms or made major mental health changes through exercise. The best thing is that the benefits of sport come at any age. The younger you are, the better habits you'll develop, but you just need to start.

Move Your Mind with Peter: Start a healthy living and exercise program

Find an activity you enjoy and begin slowly with gradual build-up. Try to do some sort of easy activity, such as a simple walking program, on alternate days each week. The ultimate target is up to 150 minutes per week of some type of cardiac (aerobic) movement. In the early days, this amount can be less as you gradually build up a regular routine.

Aim to include these components of a well-balanced exercise program:

- *Aerobic activity.* Use large muscle groups in a consistent, rhythmic manner. This can include walking, cycling, rowing, skipping, an elliptical walker, stair climber, or even running that you build up.

- *Strength training.* This helps build muscle tone, helping with strength and posture, as well as fatigue, and assists with preventing falls and aids balance.

- *Flexibility.* Stretching with floor exercises or yoga will assist to promote joint range motion and better activity performance.

- *Nutrition advice.* A healthy eating program will assist in providing optimal fuel for the body as well as the recovery ingredients needed after workouts.

Frequency

Start with three session per week, aiming to build up to five or six sessions.

Intensity

Moderate effort means you can hold a conversation while exercising, but the intensity should be hard enough so that you can't sing!

Type

Any activity using large muscle groups will provide aerobic benefits, but it's important to mix up your activities to give different muscles a chance to work over the course of the week.

Time

Initially, begin with 10- to 15-minute sessions, gradually building up to 30 minutes per day with an ultimate target of 150 minutes per week. The 30 minutes can be cumulative, for example 3 × 10-minute exercise bursts.

Benefits of exercise

Dr Susan Cheng of Harvard-affiliated Brigham and Women's Hospital says, 'I often tell my patients that if we had the ability to put what exactly exercise does for us into a pill, it would be worth a million dollars. The irony is, of course, that exercise itself is actually free'.

This is such a great statement. When it comes to our mental and physical health, there are so many things to consider. They're complicated, multi-faceted and, as we've learned, don't come with a one-stop solution.

But it's also a handy reminder of the simple and mostly free benefits that come with exercise. Almost all of us can do a form of exercise, whether it's going for a walk or jog, doing some push-ups, dancing, going for a hike—there are unlimited options available no matter where you are, no matter how much time you have and no matter what your budget is.

Exercise can help with your mind and body wellness because it:

- slows ageing

- helps treat depression

- reduces the risk of heart attacks and strokes

- improves memory and brain function

- enhances sleep quality

- helps maintain a healthy weight

- lowers blood pressure

- improves mood

- lowers cholesterol

- increases life span

- improves sexual health.

Key learnings

When you commit to moving your mind, there are a few things to remember.

1. *Don't let emotional barriers stop you.* There are a lot of emotional barriers to work out. Negative beliefs about our physical ability make it harder to get to the gym, dance class or swimming pool and experience that post-workout glow. It's also easy to give up on a living room workout, especially if nobody is there to catch you slacking off. Many people quit because they feel their best attempts are so far from 'good enough' that they give up and save themselves from the shame and embarrassment of never getting any better.

   But rather than look for reasons why you can't exercise, start looking for reasons why you can. If you can reframe your thinking from putting constant pressure on yourself and telling yourself that you're not good enough, to simply reminding yourself that any progress is positive, you'll go a long way.

   It doesn't matter if you only do five minutes on some days — anything is better than nothing. I get that life is unpredictable and you can't always find the time or energy.

2. *Be your own cheerleader!* We all have a body. Even if you don't think you're a sporty person, your body can be trained to move in many ways over time. Consider this: babies flop over (and over and over) before they build enough strength to sustain a crawl. Sometimes they get frustrated, tired and overwhelmed, and then comes the

(continued)

93

inevitable: 'Hello tantrum!' But an encouraging parent will celebrate the tiniest bit of progress like it's the most fabulous event since The Big Bang.

3. *Encourage yourself.* If your progress is slow and it's getting you down, be an encouraging parent to yourself. Practise self-encouragement because unless you have unlimited money and can afford full-time trainers to motivate you, the only sustainable way to get long-term results is through 'you'. After all, in life we can get beaten up. We fail at things, have our hearts broken and fall flat on our faces. You can either let this break you and prevent your growth, or you can remind yourself that failure is a part of life and it's how you learn.

   An unfortunate part of growing up is that the passion and blind faith we have as kids often gets beaten out of us. Be aware of this and fight against it. Don't let the negative thoughts overpower you, and remind yourself that you can do it.

4. *Start small.* Start with a routine that's even quicker and easier than you think you can handle and repeat it for a minimum of 21 days to create a new habit. This applies to every new habit that you want to create. Always start small, with baby steps, and build from there.

   Whatever you set out to do, your mind jumps to the end picture before you even take the first step. If so, you're not alone. Starting something new can be overwhelming, as obviously there are many things that need to be completed to get to the end point. Instead, change your mindset to focus on each step, and enjoy each step. You can keep your end goal in mind, but if you also focus on and enjoy each step, the result will become less relevant.

5. *Put your phone away.* When you're about to start an exercise session, put your phone away. Or if you're using it for music, put a soundtrack on and don't check your messages! This will give you not only the amazing benefits

of exercise, but also a much-needed break from work and technology.

6. *Be present.* Exercise is a fantastic way to remain present. Whether you're competing in a sport or going for a run, if you push yourself during exercise, you'll force your mind into the present moment. This is because when you're hyper-focused on a strenuous activity, you take away the power from your mind to think about anything else.

   Meditation practices and mindfulness techniques are also great for this, as we'll discuss in chapter 8, 'Still Your Mind'. These don't suit everyone and if you do find it hard to still your mind, you can try strenuous or focused exercise instead as a fantastic alternative.

   Find an activity that requires your focus, such as a team sport, or do something at a super high intensity, like circuit training or a fast jog, and you'll find you're able to put a lot of your worries at bay. It's always a fantastic feeling post-exercise when you allow yourself to do this.

7. *Remember that you'll never regret exercising.* I always tell people that there are many things you'll regret when it comes to your health ... getting drunk, overeating, worrying for no reason ... But you'll never regret going out and exercising, and you'll always leave feeling better too.

8. *Take that first step.* The hardest part with exercise is getting started. Often, your mind will tell you stories such as, 'I'm too tired', 'I'm too depressed' or 'This is pointless'. When your mind starts telling you these stories, don't cave in but take it as a sign that you need to get moving and snap yourself out of your slump.

   The actual process of exercising is never as hard as taking that first step of getting dressed, packing your gym bag or stepping into the gym and picking up your first weight.

(continued)

So, think no further than that first step because once you get moving the rest will flow and become easier, and even enjoyable. I can think of countless days when I've felt anxious, exhausted, overwhelmed, depressed or had a complete lack of motivation, and literally had to will myself to move. It's always incredibly hard to start in those situations, but I can safely say that after almost 20 years of exercise, I'm yet to have an experience where I've felt mentally worse after a session. You just need to take the first ... little ... step.

9. *Avoid over-exerting yourself at the start.* It's much easier to plan and complete an easy, quick workout each day than a long, intimidating routine mapped out for months in advance. At this stage, repetition is more important than difficulty because, as I mentioned above, it takes 21 days for your brain to 're-wire' and include a new behaviour as a habit. Again, focus on the process, not the outcome. Make workouts fun, get creative, get others around you to offer support and use some of our suggested workouts!

10. *Increase the difficulty.* After 21 days, you'll have set a foundational habit for daily movement, and this is when you can start to increase the length and difficulty of your workouts and push yourself towards ambitious goals. If you can stick to your new exercise routine, chances are you'll naturally increase the degree of difficulty once it starts to become a habit. This will empower you, boost your self-esteem and leave you wanting to continually challenge yourself. Plus, you'll start to feel and look different — great for body positivity. Always remind yourself that the hardest part of anything is simply starting. Whenever things are tough, repeat the mantra that if you stick to it, things will always improve!

11. *Appreciate those endorphins!* By this time, you'll be feeling the benefits of exercise: increased focus and lifted mood

thanks to all the additional endorphins produced by working out. This can become a little addictive, take it from me, but if you're going to become addicted to anything, exercise is a pretty good one! I want exercise to become as much a part of your day as sleep, eating and drinking. Make it one of the key parts of your day that you look forward to and really value.

12. *Consider your diet.* There are so many different diet styles out there: Paleo, Atkins, 5:2, plant-based ... the list goes on. Before committing to one form of eating at the exclusion of others, research the benefits and risks associated with each thoroughly. Test recipes and find out what works for your lifestyle. Set realistic, achievable goals to incorporate healthier food into your lifestyle gradually, while removing or limiting unhealthy foods. We'll go into this in the second pathway, Feed Your Mind.

13. *Keep it balanced.* Over time, physical activity, sleep, hydration, meditation and nutrition have a cumulative positive impact on both your physical and mental health. There is no 'one size fits all', but generally it's best to keep a balance when it comes to your health. Exercise without eating, sleeping and hydrating properly will be much less impactful. Keep a balance and make sure you're doing the right things to support your exercise routine.

14. *When in doubt, remember:* physical and mental health go hand in hand. A good-feeling body supports a good-feeling mind and vice versa. The same is true in reverse: a body that feels tired, weak and uncomfortable can be a real downer on your mood. Look after both with a sustainable ritual of healthy physical and emotional choices.

When you consider these points, it's profound how beneficial exercise is for our minds and bodies. I think if you take the time to let this sink in, you might make fewer excuses and find more ways to make exercise a part of your daily life. Even five minutes of movement each day is better than nothing.

Here are some examples of easy ways to exercise and get moving each day:

- going for a walk with a friend

- walking or running games

- ball sports such as soccer and football

- throwing a frisbee

- taking your dog to the park

- having a walking meeting

- taking work calls while going for a walk

- hiking

- skipping

- online yoga classes

- virtual workouts with friends

- going to your local gym

- bike riding

- team sports.

The key is to find a way to make exercise part of your everyday life because daily movement, coupled with proper nutrition, are together considered beneficial antidepressant aids. It's not about making massive overhauls of your diet and lifestyle; rather make small, sustained changes to incorporate more exercise and healthy practices into your life, which can make dramatic changes to your mindset and performance.

INSIGHTS FROM SAM WOOD

Sam Wood is an Australian health and fitness expert who has a popular exercise and fitness program called '28 by Sam Wood'. I have followed Sam's career for several years, and watched him become one of the leading fitness experts in the world. He has a down-to-earth and relatable approach that can help anyone.

I think exercise is critical for so many reasons. A lot of people start exercising because they're on a weight-loss mission or they want to look good, but it's the other benefits that often surprise people the most and keep people going. I think this is very much the physical and mental feeling, helping to pump endorphins, improving mood and energy levels, helping you sleep better, giving you more clarity, and making you a better person at home and at work. An outside workout gives you vitamin D and fresh air with an after-workout endorphin rush that makes you happier and has a far greater impact on you than perhaps you thought. The list of benefits is endless.

Personally, I'm a big fan of moving in the morning. I have a long drive to work each day and leave at 7 am, so I make sure to get up at 5.30 am and go for a run with the dog, or a swim or whatever. Anything to get the blood pumping and moving. These days it's not about getting a six pack, or lower body fat or other crap I worried about in my 20s. It's more about improving mood, energy, productivity and sleep. We love to put things off

(continued)

and move the goalposts, but just get up and get it done in the morning. I reckon it's a total game changer!

My personal challenge is trying to slow down. I'm always go, go, go, so whether it's finding five minutes of stillness, reflecting a bit or just patting myself on the back for achieving goals, I have to force myself to find balance and also enjoy the moment. Therefore, I like to start the day fast and finish the day slow.

Something else I've noticed is that I think a lot of people think that those who exercise are magically motivated, or something. I can categorically tell you that no-one is magically motivated: habit or routine is what you should strive for. There is no golden rule, either. If it's a battle to get up at 6 am, maybe that's not the answer for you. Not everyone has to have a two-minute freezing cold shower, and not everybody has to meditate for 10 minutes at the start of the day. You have to find what works for you because you're fighting yourself every single day. Don't be demotivated by switching it up and trying something else. And don't let people tell you one thing is better than the other — it's what's right for you.

When it comes to mental health, I'm conscious about not saying to people that all will be fixed in your life if you just go to the gym because, of course, it's just not that simple. That's not to say you don't need to do other things to address mental health issues, but there have been almost zero occasions where I have seen people introduce exercise that hasn't helped their mental health. For some, it's the complete answer and in others absolutely a step in the right direction. I'm always amazed how many people experiencing mental health issues aren't exercising, and this would absolutely be one of the first places that I would start. Then, taking care of yourself from a nutrition and sleep perspective would follow on from that.

My message is to find what works for you. I get questions like 'Sam, what's better: running or HIIT or yoga or...?' It's important to find whatever works for you, that you enjoy and will be able to do consistently. If you try seven different options, there should be two or three that you like the most. There's a saying in the gym industry that I like in relation to personal trainers who put a television on the treadmill: 'it's about making the medicine taste better'. We all know that exercise is good for us and we all know we should do it. Find what works for you that makes the medicine taste better.

In my business, 28 by Sam Wood, we live by two sayings. The first is 'progress, not perfection'. Don't try and do it all, and don't try to be it all. Don't deprive yourself of your favourite foods or feel like you have to train for an hour every day. The second is 'share, don't compare'. Share your successes and be proud of what you're achieving, but it's your journey. Instagram is having a negative impact because you're always worrying about these unrealistic, fabricated and manipulated snapshot posts of someone else's life. With social media bombarding us, it's easier said than done and hard to switch off, but you do need to be strong enough to ask yourself, 'Is the time I'm spending on social media, or even the face-to-face group of friends I'm comparing myself to, hurting me?' If it's hurting you, you need to address it. Stay strong!

Move Your Mind with Sam: MITM (Move in the Morning)

- Awaken your body and brain in the morning with whatever form of exercise works for you. It doesn't need to be long or intense—just enough to get the blood pumping and endorphins flowing to increase energy and mood.

- Set yourself a 28-day goal. Too often we set goals that are too big, unrealistic or too far away: 28 days is the perfect goal-setting period. It's long enough to see results, but close enough that you keep your eye on the prize.

Creating a habit

If you want to make exercise a bigger part of your life, create a habit out of it. As I mentioned earlier, they say psychologically it takes around 21 days to make or break a habit. So, if you can keep this in mind when approaching exercise, your chance of sustained success will dramatically increase. I can't tell you how many times over the years friends have asked me for advice on creating a fitness routine for them. The main thing I always tell them is to create a habit and not worry about getting quick results. Most of the time this advice gets ignored and they go all in on the new fitness endeavour. There's the initial excitement and enthusiasm, which usually doesn't last long before progress comes to a halt. Pushing yourself too hard at the beginning also programs your mind to associate pain with exercise.

The key is to start out with some really basic goals and be easy on yourself. If you go too hard too early you'll burn out before you even stick to it long enough to form a habit. You can increase the degree of difficulty over time—at the beginning all that matters is that you enjoy the process and keep doing it long enough for it to start forming into a habit. This applies to any new habit you're looking to form. We'll cover more on habits in part IV.

Daily routines are an incredibly important part of my life. As I outlined in chapter 1, exercise is probably the most important part of my life and I really believe movement is one of the best things we can do for our wellbeing. It was easily one of the best things I could do for myself from an early age, and it's one of the key activities I associate with having a clear and healthy mind and body.

I have a highly competitive sports background, and I still train every day. I've made this into a habit as much as eating and sleeping are part of my day—and I'm better for it. I also mediate every morning (I learned transcendental meditation many years ago and have been doing it ever since), write a morning gratitude list and do breathing exercises. Acting is also such an important part of this routine. Routines are incredibly important to have in place for when something unexpected happens.

My approach

Growing up, I was lucky to have incredible support from my Uncle Bruce—my dad's sister's husband. From a very early age, Uncle Bruce saw something of himself in me: obsession, passion and an unwillingness to conform. Like me, Bruce had trained to be an elite athlete and later developed a passion for acting and performing. He'd had his own problems with addiction, which he overcame, and would always go against convention. He refused to be anyone other than himself. Seeing that I was sport obsessed from a young age, I think he recognised that I needed guidance on how to channel my mind into positive things.

He would often come around three to four nights a week after work to train with me and we would practise one on one for hours on the football field. He would take me to all my games and will me on. He did the same when I was training to be a middle-distance runner and more recently, was the biggest advocate and support regarding my acting career.

Uncle Bruce constantly fed me with positive affirmations. He would tell me that I could achieve at the highest level and make it if I just chose to focus and put in the work. When things got hard, or I doubted myself, he would always tell me that I had what it took and that I'd eventually get there if I stuck at it.

This had a profound impact on me at the time, and an even bigger lasting effect. It burned a message into my mind that it's okay to be myself, follow my dreams and fuel my passions. It gave meaning and support to what I stood for and provided a backbone to achieve them.

Sadly, Bruce got sick some years ago with a motor neurone disease, which slowly made him lose all motor abilities. He recently passed away, but even watching how he hung on for 10 years when the doctors gave him two is an example of how powerful the mind is. I carry a picture of Bruce and myself in my wallet with the message, 'Do it for Bruce', and I look at it every time I doubt myself and start to lose hope. It's enough to spark me back into line. His impact has been forever lasting on me and has given me unlimited fuel to back myself.

I can't be clearer on how important it is to have positive mentors like my Uncle Bruce in your life. As I touched on earlier, the world can be tough and you're often told you're not good enough. Kids start out being open-minded and genuinely passionate and excited about life, yet this gets beaten out of them through hardship.

However, if you have positive mentors who remind you of your own value and ultimately teach you to believe in yourself, this goes a long, long way. I've been very lucky to have many of these people in my life, and it's given me great self-esteem towards sticking to, and achieving, my goals.

My experience of exercise through athletics is another example of how positive mentors have affected my life for the better.

I competed at state and national levels in middle-distance running and was at one point the state champion in cross-country running. As with Bruce, I had an incredible coach and mentor in Alan Gittens. At the time, Alan was retired, but athletics was his lifelong passion and he would take in a few athletes for training. He never charged anyone for his expertise, but the lucky few of us he trained received his unconditional support. We would train four nights a week and compete on weekends and he would be there for every session and competition. He would push me because he could see I wanted to be tested, but ultimately, it was his passion that I most learned from him.

Alan had a deep passion for middle-distance running. He would tell us stories about famous Australian runners, the lengths they went to in training and how far they would push themselves to get results. There was a richness in the way he talked about it that taught me how important it is in life to care deeply about things.

He was retired and dedicating huge parts of his life to this for free, but he could not have been happier. I remember a quote I learned from Alan that has stuck with me to this day: 'A runner must run with dreams in his heart, not money in his pocket'. It was a quote from Emil Zatopek, one of the all-time distance-running greats. I often think of this quote and relate it to whatever decision I am making in my life. Am I doing something just for money or am I doing it for passion? I think it's important to continually ask yourself these questions as we can very easily get caught up in just going through the motions. The discipline and passion that Alan taught me has been one of the most important experiences I have had and again, they were fostered through sport and exercise.

Another hero of mine as a kid was the runner Steve Prefontaine. He was an outspoken American middle-distance runner at a time when the sport was still amateur. He was also the original ambassador for Nike. His coach, Bill Bowerman, co-founded the company with Phil Knight, where they literally produced the initial waffle running shoes on a waffle iron.

Prefontaine (or Pre, as he was known) was larger than life and had the 'X factor'. He could attract anyone's attention and had no fear, refusing to follow norms. He put middle-distance running on the map and turned his signature 5k race into a spectacle, transforming a sport that was previously seen as boring. Compared to other runners, he had little natural talent and refused to follow convention and pace out his races. Instead, he'd go flat out from start to finish claiming 'somebody may beat me, but you are going to have to bleed to do it'.

His message was to follow your heart and face fear head on, no matter the consequences. He had a great quote too: 'To give anything less than the best is to sacrifice the gift'. He said it's okay to fail, but you should always follow your heart and give your best.

Sadly, Pre died in a car crash at 24 after his first Olympic games. But his larger than life personality touched people all over the world, with Hollywood films made about him, such as *Without Limits*, produced by Tom Cruise and starring Billy Crudup as Pre.

The joy of movement

I can still remember the pure joy of playing with my friends as a kid. There was no incentive—just great fun outside exploring, inventing games or kicking a ball around. We would play for hours until it got too dark or we had to go home, and then count down the hours until we could go out and play again.

I always remind myself of this and make sure I can find a way to enjoy exercise. Sometimes it can feel tedious, as I often train alone, but there's always a way to make it enjoyable. I try to use the time to declutter my mind. I always try to put my phone away and let my mind clear itself, have some downtime and immerse myself in the activity.

If I'm in the middle of a challenging session, I'll focus on how amazing I'll feel at the end and that's what drives me through it. On the other hand, if it's boring, I'll break it down and focus on finishing one rep at a time until it's over. This goes back to the key learning of taking it one step at a time and focusing on the process rather than the outcome. It always leaves my mind feeling amazing and clear too.

During the COVID-19 pandemic, my ability to exercise was tested. Like many, I had no access to a gym or equipment. I've always had bad knees from my running days, so I was even more limited.

Rather than let this get me down or use it as an excuse, I looked at it as a challenge to learn new training routines.

I spent hours and hours looking up and testing at-home training sessions and eventually developed a range of high-intensity circuits, which were more difficult than some of the previous sessions I was doing and would increase my fitness level. I then created a daily training group with a bunch of friends from all over the world. We would all jump online, and I would run everyone through the session. This became really rewarding, leading me to reconnect with friends I hadn't spoken to in years, motivating me to train with a group and making me feel fantastic seeing how much it was also helping everyone involved. This eventually led to daily Instagram Live sessions during lockdown, which was also something I wouldn't have done otherwise. We can find the positive in every situation if we allow ourselves to.

A final word

Exercise has been one of the most important things in my life. Without it, there is no way I would be where I am today. From the joy of simple play as a kid, to training to be a professional athlete and later using exercise as a crutch to cope during times of uncertainty, exercise has shaped my whole life.

Getting your body moving is one of the most natural things you can do. If you watch kids, they are constantly on the move, exploring and inventing games. It's a beautiful part of life. Somewhere and somehow along the way this gets drummed out of us and we often don't find a way back to incorporate it in our lives.

I feel fortunate that I have prioritised exercise in my life over the years. Through the help of my mentors and coaches, and by learning and feeling the daily benefits, it has remained a daily part of my life. I hope by writing this that I can encourage and inspire you to also make it a part of your life, and to find what works for you to create a healthy and happy future.

Move Your Mind with Nick:
Start small

- *Create a simple and sustainable exercise routine.* Start small — even five minutes a day is enough in the beginning. Your goal is not to get quick fitness results; this is a habit-building exercise! There is no one method or routine you should do, so mix it up. If a lack of time, money or transport is an obstacle to going to the gym, create a workout you can do in your living room. Think sit-ups, lunges, push-ups, star-jumps and skipping on the spot. Start with five minutes.

- *Join a local sporting club.* It's a great way to meet new people and feel motivated by those around you. It will keep you accountable and be a great outlet from your regular routine. If you're nervous about starting, or don't think that you will stick to it, ask a friend to hold you accountable and encourage you to stick it out.

- *Use the internet to your advantage.* Google the workouts you want to try, go onto YouTube and look up exercises and find what works for you. There's an abundance of free content available and if you have the patience to look through it, you can find a lot of great information.

EATING HEALTHY IS THE
BEST MEDICINE EVER.
FRESH INGREDIENTS HAVE
BEEN PUT ON THIS PLANET
SO WE CAN LOOK AFTER
OUR HEALTH.

Manu Feildel

CHAPTER 6

PATHWAY 2:
FEED YOUR MIND

My second pathway to better mental health is all about food and nutrition, and the way these affect your mental health. When you feed your body, you're also feeding your mind, and vice versa. If you don't feed your mind on a mental level, are overwhelmed, or consuming too much negative information and not thinking clearly, you're unlikely to eat well. And if you're not physically feeding yourself properly, it's likely to affect your mental clarity, leading to poor decisions or simply feeling sluggish.

Importantly, I use the term Feed Your Mind to encompass the content and information we consume too, which is critical to wellbeing. If you're glued to screens every day and consuming never-ending content from newsfeeds and social media, this can greatly affect your mental wellbeing. We're already seeing this play out with well-documented stories of people affected by negative aspects of social media, such as trolling.

In this chapter, I'll explore our relationship with nutrition and food. I'll take you through some of the science behind eating, common problems around nutrition and the most popular diets, and then give you some tasks to help you set up positive food habits in your life.

Food and our mental health

The close relationship between food and mood means that our choice of foods and dietary patterns can play a role in the way we feel. The food we eat affects our glycaemia (the amount of sugar or glucose in the blood), our immunity and the gut biome, as we'll learn later in the chapter.

However, scientists and nutritionists need to conduct more research to fully understand the mechanics linking food to mental wellbeing, and particularly how good nutrition can improve mental health.

Knowing that making changes to your diet will improve your mental wellbeing is just the first step. Acting on this is more difficult—there are so many barriers to push through. A big one for many is that when you're struggling, junk food can become a crutch, and can be used as a coping mechanism to deal with mental health issues. Financial constraints also play a big part in this. My message is that you can only do what you can do, so the main thing is to be aware of this and try to take small steps forward.

Here are some key factors to look at when it comes to food and our mood.

- *Carbohydrates:* processed carbohydrates can greatly affect mood and lead to depression and anxiety. Carbohydrates turn to sugar and fat and have a big impact on insulin levels, which cause changes in mood and can also lead to issues such as diabetes.

- *Inflammatory foods:* Foods that are high in sugar and refined carbohydrates are examples of inflammatory foods. These foods cause spikes in mood and can cause health problems such as obesity.

- *Gut biome:* In recent years, the link between the brain, gut and microbiome has become more popular. The 'gut microbiome' or 'gut bugs' comprise the trillions of microorganisms and their genetic material that live in the intestinal tract. They are critical to health, wellbeing and the way your body processes important functions, including absorbing what you eat, metabolism, weight and mood. As a result, gut biome has become more researched as new evidence mounts, with inflammation of the gut linked to mental health issues such as anxiety and depression. The upshot is that mental health is not narrowly located in the head, but in the physical body and the natural world. The 'gut-brain axis' is a relatively new term that describes this.

PATHWAY 2 FEED YOUR MIND

INSIGHTS FROM DR JOANNA MCMILLAN

Dr Joanna McMillan is one of Australia's best-known nutrition and lifestyle specialists. I was researching leading nutritionists to interview for the book and Joanna's name came up as a presenter, author and nutrition consultant. I reached out and she was kind enough to allow me to interview her on the podcast and to contribute to the book. She is a real leader in her field and offers the latest information and research on nutrition.

I have been researching the influence of food and lifestyle on brain health for a long time. When I started my career 20 years ago, we had this idea that the brain was lucid and just functions without our control. Research over the past decade has shown

(continued)

us that we actually have a huge influence over how healthy our brain is and how it functions day to day. This includes mood!

What we know now is that there are huge links between gut problems and anxiety and depression. There are links between diet (especially the Mediterranean diet, which has been well studied in relation to mental health), exercise, time outdoors, and getting among nature to improve mental health.

Further to that is the research behind the gut biome, microbiome and the link to mental health — it's mind blowing the research currently coming out. I was the host of a three-part series on Australia's ABC channel called *Gut Revolution*, where we interviewed people from all over the world: microbiologists, biologists, nutritionists and scientists. While they all offered different angles, there was a common link to what we call the gut-brain axis, a communication highway between the gut and the brain. We always knew that diet was important for mental health, but we didn't know why. We now understand that things like fibres help fuel the microbiome and it's actually the products of that fermentation that are influencing brain function — which is pretty out there! We are also learning about what else is in food, like phytochemicals, which are plant chemicals. It raises a question: if we can change an adult's microbiome to make it healthier, can we become more mentally resilient?

This focus on nutrition science is still relatively young: how can you trust nutrition scientists when the thinking seems to change every week?

As for me, I see diet in two parts: education (which in lifestyle medicine must be evidence-based) and teaching people how to put these changes into practice. If you are depressed it's very difficult to jump out of bed excited to prepare a healthy meal. It's about baby steps. Making small holistic changes to not just your diet, but all areas of health over time. If you can take small steps, the bigger changes will come.

Personally, I'm a fan of intermittent fasting. We are surrounded by food 24/7 so it can be good to give your gut a break. Research is supporting this and demonstrating that it plays a potential role in turning on your longevity gene and helping with weight loss. But like everything, this approach isn't for everyone. If you have low blood sugar, for example, it's unlikely right for you. It's about understanding that there's no one healthy way of eating, having a holistic approach and eating real foods. It's about looking at all of the options and deciding what can work best for you and getting those core foundations right.

Nobody questions that some people are better off walking or doing yoga to strengthen their core. Nobody thinks twice about the personalisation of exercise. Yet somehow, we find it hard to get our heads around diet. A lot of diets can become cultish—people find a certain diet and put on their blinkers, thinking it's the only solution. Your diet should be personalised to your own likes and dislikes, how much you exercise / how many calories you burn. It's about what works specifically for you—and there is no one set formula.

Again, small steps are what I believe will help people. Find what works for you with simple things like getting outdoors, getting vitamin D on your skin and exercise, all of which are important. There are so many avenues to consider, but recognise that improving your diet, like all areas of health, takes challenging behaviour change, so ensure you get the support you need.

PATHWAY 2
FEED YOUR MIND

Move Your Mind with Joanna: Focus on nutrition

- Aim for 30 different whole-plant foods across your week.

- Limit or cut out ultra-processed foods and drinks—that is, those with an ingredients list full of already highly processed ingredients and lots of things you may not even recognise as foods!

- Sit down at the kitchen bench or table to eat all your meals without other distractions like the television or your computer. This helps to promote mindful (rather than mindless) eating so that you eat to your body's satiety cues, and enjoy it too!

The impact of nutrition on our mental health

For many of us, food is life. Nutrition and eating are the ways we love to live, entertain and socialise. They represent the way we nurture our bodies, but equally, they create indulgence and pleasure.

Which food camp are you in? Unprocessed, organic and locally produced meat, fruit and vegetables? Fast food and microwave meals all the way? Or something in-between? There's no judgement here! We're all about understanding your food levers so you can get to grips a little better with what's happening under your skin. It doesn't help that a steady flow of advertising on the right, wrong, best and worst diets floods our inboxes and letterboxes every day.

For many of us, issues around food are extremely complex. They can stem from a difficult relationship with eating in childhood, and they can last for life. They can be so severe that they can cause serious health conditions such as anorexia or obesity. Tragically, they can cost lives too.

Food habits in the Western world

A lot of health issues in the Western world stem from poor diet; more specifically, a reliance on fast food. High in fat, sugar, salt and carbohydrates, fast food is a huge part of many of our diets, where it's popularly used for comfort out of necessity and/or for simple convenience. For example, if people are struggling financially, the cheaper and easier option often involves eating food that is lacking in nutrition. On the other hand, the most expensive options are organic, but this isn't a viable option for many people. Rather than choose foods that fuel our bodies and look after our health, we fall back on bad choices and vices that are all readily available, and it often works to our detriment. Educating and disciplining ourselves on how we can eat better and make it part of our routine is a great way to get around these issues.

Let's take a look at the most common food-related conditions.

Comfort eating and obesity

Comfort eating is very common for many people and often becomes an addiction. But we don't often associate food with addiction because it's a core part of our daily lives. In fact, it's because of this that food is so addictive. For example, if you have a problem with alcohol you can go cold turkey and not look back. If you have a food addiction, you still need to eat every day to function.

It's a tricky balance to control an addiction when you still need to physically eat. But it's something we need to address because global obesity has more than tripled since 1975. More education around this moving forward is critical.

According to the WHO:

about 13% of the world's adult population (11% of men and 15% of women) were obese ... Most of the world's population live in countries where overweight and obesity kills more people than underweight ... over 340 million children and adolescents aged 5–19 were overweight or obese.

Like many things that go hand-in-hand with capitalism and consumerism, the Western world encourages consumption. And lots of it. Eating habits are like all the other mental teachings and are passed down through generations. The way we interact with food and how we think about it is often passed on through parenting and other factors too. For some nationalities, feasting is part of their culture so they are accustomed to large portions and there's no such thing as eating in moderation.

Cost can also be a factor. As I mentioned, it takes time and often costs more money to source organic, healthy foods. The easier option is to buy processed, fatty foods that are cheap and filling. It takes less time, and is cheaper, but ultimately doesn't lead to anything positive. Our mindset is so important when it comes to diet. If we're feeling down, we're more likely to make poor decisions around food.

Diabetes

Diabetes is a health issue that is becoming a big problem around the world. It occurs when the body doesn't produce enough insulin or cannot effectively use the insulin it produces. Basically, diabetes occurs as type 1 and type 2; the former is typically diagnosed in childhood or young adulthood and requires daily insulin. Type 2 is related more to lifestyle factors, and it's this form of diabetes that can be managed—and often prevented—in many cases by making daily changes such as exercising and eating well.

Here's what the WHO says about diabetes:

- From 1980 to 2014 the prevalence of diabetes rose from 108 million to 422 million people globally.

- In 2016, approximately 1.6 million people died of diabetes.

- Diabetes was arguably the seventh leading cause of death in 2016.

- Diabetes is a major cause of stroke, heart attack, kidney failure, blindness and lower limb amputation.

- Type 2 diabetes can be prevented or delayed by adopting a healthy diet, regular physical activity, maintaining a good body weight and not smoking.

The health impacts associated with diabetes are enormous and are largely a result of our unhealthy lifestyles. With so much being easy and convenient, we walk and move much less than we used to, eat more sugars and more unhealthy foods and don't drink enough water.

Fasting

There is increasing scientific evidence around the health benefits of fasting. While it has been around for a long time, it's grown popular in recent years, as evidenced in the insights we gleaned from Dr Joanna McMillan, who is a fan. Fasting gives the body a break from eating and putting energy towards processing foods, giving it a chance to repair cells and conserve energy.

As you'll read later in the chapter, in the section on the 5:2 diet, intermittent fasting is another popular method. It involves periods daily of no eating and often spending 16 hours per day without consuming food. For example, stopping eating at night (around 8 pm) and not eating again until 12 pm the next day—essentially skipping breakfast. It's gained popularity because unlike diets where you need to prepare special meals, or shakes, or buy meals, you simply fast without having to buy or do anything extra.

There are many benefits associated with fasting, and it's easy to manage and maintain due to the simplicity of just skipping one meal. There's a lot of stigma around fasting as we've traditionally been taught that breakfast is the most important meal of the day. But a lot of traditional learning is now being challenged by science.

I don't think you should choose what is right or wrong, but rather educate yourself so you can make informed decisions.

Sugar

Some years ago I was lucky enough to interview Australian actor and director Damon Gameau, who made *That Sugar Film*. He's made a huge impact educating the public about the dangers that come with eating too much sugar.

Here are some of his key points:

- Sugar is an inflammatory food.

- We should be encouraging kids to eat slow-releasing foods such as eggs rather than sugary breakfast cereals.

- Fasting is not for everyone. Find what diet works for you.

- There are many kinds of fats—some are good and some are bad. Be aware of the good fats and understand that certain fats are important for our bodies.

- Gut bacteria (gut biome) is linked to our health and has a profound impact on our mental health. We can improve our gut biome through fermented foods.

- Be aware of hidden or added sugars in foods as they are not necessary and are not good for us.

- Non-alcoholic fatty liver disease is now found in more than one billion people, despite not even having a name 30 years ago. Eating sugar-based foods and too many carbohydrates will lead to diseases such as this.

- Type 2 diabetes kills someone every six seconds around the world.

- Sugar causes depression. We need to acknowledge the direct link between the foods we eat and our mental health.

Starvation / anorexia nervosa

Anorexia is categorised by having a distorted body image with an unwanted fear of being overweight. This manifests in depriving the body of food.

Anorexia and related disorders stem from a mental health disorder. By the same token, they can stem from another extreme, such as extreme body building, where you feel inadequate and lose sight of the muscle you're putting on. In the same way other addictions work, your mind uses the situation as a catalyst to deal with deeper problems.

There are two main types of anorexia:

- *restricting:* this is the predominant type where people severely restrict the amount of food intake

- *binge eating and purging:* this can involve binge eating and then using different methods to vomit up the food.

Anorexia and related disorders are serious mental health disorders that require professional help.

**PATHWAY 2
FEED YOUR MIND**

INSIGHTS FROM MANU FEILDEL

French-Australian chef Manu Feildel is a restaurateur and television personality best known as a judge and co-host on the successful series My Kitchen Rules *and* Australia's Got Talent. *Manu and I also competed on the reality show* Dancing with the Stars *back in 2011 and stayed in touch over the years, following each other's careers. He has an incredible story and was the first person I thought of for Feed Your Mind.*

There's a strong correlation between what you eat and your mental health. If you are underweight, or overweight, you are likely to be mentally unwell. Therefore, eating healthy is the best medicine ever. Fresh ingredients have been put on this planet so you can look after your health. Additionally, it's important animals are fed the right diet — if they have the wrong diet, you will be eating the wrong meat.

(continued)

I honestly think there is only one diet we should follow — to eat fresh foods and use fresh ingredients in moderation. Read labels if it's in a packet and if it's in the freezer or has been on the shelf for two years, question it. Make sure it's fresh and organic. Fresh food was available over 100 years ago, but now we're offered cheap, unhealthy alternatives. Unfortunately, organic is expensive, sometimes making it hard to eat that way.

Alcohol is another thing. Yes, sometimes we can't avoid it (I find it hard to stay off it over Christmas), but when I had a month off drinking, I felt better mentally, could sleep better and could concentrate more.

Also, there can be a lot of poison in food. Sugar and stuff like that is bad for your guts. If it's bad for your guts, it's bad for your mind.

Not long ago I did a 12-week program and lost weight, but it wasn't sustainable. For me it's all balance. You can still eat pizza but just not every night. Cooking is my life, so I want to enjoy food, but you need balance. And exercise keeps me mentally sane and allows me to occasionally treat myself.

It's hard to follow a diet long term and we usually get to a point where we say, 'I have had enough' and go back to old habits. Everyone has an excuse: 'I don't have time', 'I am too busy', 'I can't afford it'. But if it's important, you can make time, get up earlier and find healthy, affordable food. It's like a dog chasing its tail — if you don't eat well, you are not well mentally, don't sleep well, you drink alcohol, and so on.

It doesn't help when every couple of decades we get fed different messages about food. We were told fat was not good (but it depends on which fats). Now, we are told animal fats are good and sugars are bad. What I am saying is, let's go back to common sense. Have a burger, but don't use tomato sauce (it's full of sugar), and make sure you have salad with it to get enough nutrients. Keep things simple. Use common sense — don't drink a bottle of Coke at 9 am when you are thirsty! You can't teach common sense but maybe by communicating and educating about improving our diets we can. It's crazy we have to keep educating but let's keep on doing it!

Move Your Mind with Manu: Keep it real

- Eat real food, which means real ingredients and nothing processed with all sorts of preservatives or things that are addictive.

- Exercise is as important as food and if you exercise a little bit every day and eat good food, you'll feel on top of the world.

- Less alcohol and more water are obviously better for you — but all I'd say is in moderation!

PATHWAY 2
FEED YOUR MIND

Popular diets

We all know we could eat better foods. But when there are so many diets, healthy eating plans, meal plans and regimes to choose from, it can be hard to know where to start. In this section, I want to break down the most popular approaches to food and dieting so that you can make an informed decision about which are best for you.

Let's take a closer look at some popular diets from around the world.

Paleo

What is it?
Following the Paleo diet involves eating the foods early humans did around 2.5 million years ago. It comprises a mix of fruits, nuts, meats and oils and is designed around the idea that the human body evolved on these foods and is not suited to the processed foods we eat today.

What are the benefits?
The Paleo diet often leads to weight loss, lower blood pressure and better management of appetite.

What are the risks?
The Paleo diet can be expensive as it lacks whole grains and legumes, which are much more affordable than products such as meats and nuts.

Atkins

What is it?
The Atkins diet was developed by Robert C. Atkins in the 1960s. The diet restricts the amount of carbohydrate intake, while focusing on eating proteins and fats. The main idea is to help you lose weight and keep it off over time. Like many others, this diet has evolved over time, with changes such as including eating higher fibre vegetables and accommodating vegetarian diets.

What are the benefits?
The main benefit of the Atkins diet is weight loss. It can also help with health conditions such as diabetes, heart disease and high blood pressure.

What are the risks?
Starting out, the Atkins diet can have side effects such as headaches, fatigue, dizziness and generally just feeling weak and out of energy. It's not going to suit everyone, so consult a doctor before beginning.

5:2

What is it?

As I mentioned earlier, fasting has become very popular and there's science to back up the benefits. Basically, whenever you consume food it causes inflammation as your body uses energy to process and digest it, rarely giving your body time to repair itself. Not only does fasting allow for this repair time, it also changes up your routine. If you exercised in the gym the same way each day, your body would become complacent because it knows what to expect. It's the same with food. The 5:2 diet is quite simple: five days of eating normally (a standard, healthy diet) mixed with two days of lowering your calorie intake to a quarter of your daily needs (around 500 calories for women and 600 for men). You can choose on which two days you wish to eat the minimal calories.

What are the benefits?

One of the main benefits of this diet is how easy it is to follow. Unlike many others, you don't need to spend large amounts of time worrying about getting the right ingredients and following a strict eating plan. All you need to do is stick to the two days per week of cutting your calorie intake. Other benefits include weight loss, reduction in insulin levels and decreased inflammation.

What are the risks?

This diet is not for everyone. If you have low blood sugar levels, a history of eating disorders or are pregnant, for example, it's probably not going to be suitable. It's best to consult your doctor before making a decision around the 5:2 diet and other forms of fasting.

Plant-based

What is it?

A plant-based diet involves eating foods that come mainly from plants. It doesn't necessarily mean avoiding meat and other food sources, but plant-based foods are the primary source of nutrition.

What are the benefits?

There are many benefits of a plant-based diet. The documentary *The Game Changers* is really compelling with regard to this, and it has attracted a lot of attention since it was released in 2018. Much of the benefit comes from eating less meat, as our bodies have not been designed to consume the amount of meat many of us eat daily. Eating less meat can reduce the risk of heart disease, lower cholesterol, lower obesity and reduce the chance of type 2 diabetes, among other benefits.

What are the risks?

Plant-based diets can potentially lead to a lack of protein, vitamin and mineral intake due to the lack of other food sources that can come with it. This can be combatted by consuming enough plant-based proteins, such as tofu, lentils, nuts and other similar foods. Like anything, it can benefit if managed in the right way, but equally should be approached with caution.

###

Regardless of which option speaks to you best, the great thing about food is that a lot of it comes down to common sense. And a great way to frame your thinking with food is this: what is sustainable for me in my everyday life?

As for me, what's sustainable is getting the morning started off on the right track with something that I can control. And that's my morning routine involving making a simple smoothie. I don't have a go-to recipe as such; it's more just a blend of whatever fruit and vegetables I feel like and what's readily available from the fridge. It's about getting that burst of fresh nutrition in the morning, which sets me up and is something I'm happy to repeat every day.

Key learnings

When considering your dietary needs, remember the following:

1. *Proper nutrition.* Along with daily movement, proper nutrition is considered an excellent antidepressant aid. Just as I recommended small, sustained changes for the way you move, I recommend the same approach for the way you eat. I truly believe that incorporating good, healthy food into your life can make dramatic changes to your mindset and performance.

2. *Achievable goals.* Set realistic, achievable goals to add healthier foods into your lifestyle gradually. You might have a meal plan that includes cooking 10 new recipes each week. That might be unsustainable for you, so maybe just pick a few of them, and start small, while also removing or limiting unhealthy foods. Remember, it takes 21 days for the brain to create a new habit. Starting new diets falls under that rule too.

3. *Emotional eating.* When it comes to celebrating, it's hard not to get swept up in the emotional aspect of the eating experience. And when so many of life's celebrations involve eating, it's hard to avoid. Celebrations like birthdays include cake, Ramadan includes both fasting and feasting at specific times, while Christmas and Thanksgiving are large-scale food celebrations revolving around mealtimes. It could even be something as simple as having an ice cream on a Saturday night. Sounds tasty! What I want to

(continued)

get across to you here is that enjoying food is a part of life, and it should be celebrated. I don't want you to miss out on it by becoming hyper-restrictive because that could open up a whole new can of worms. Instead, allow treats when the occasion calls for it and avoid using food as a crutch for comfort. When this urge comes on, try and replace it with something healthy such as meditation, talking to a friend or going for a walk.

4. *Portioning wisely.* This is a bit of a trap. It may seem easy to eat healthy foods throughout the day, comprising good meals that tick all the boxes. But what you need to watch is dishing up too much.

5. *Calorie counting.* You may have heard of the phrase 'calorie counting'. It's about managing the total number of calories in the food and drink that you've eaten and drunk across the day. People who manage their nutritional health will know how many calories they can consume based on their goals — fat loss, muscle gain or to maintain optimal health — and this can be a great way to monitor what you're putting into your body each day. If you're disciplined, counting calories is a great way to watch what you eat across a day. Here's another phrase you're probably familiar with: 'You are what you eat'. I believe this 100 per cent. I hold myself accountable to whatever I put in my mouth, but it's harder at particular times and I'm not always successful at following this.

6. *Choose better quality.* Where possible, choose a better quality product made with natural ingredients and fewer chemicals, preservatives and allergens. The reason I say this is because your body has an easier time processing them. That means better sleep and more improved cognitive function. But how do you know whether the food you're eating has these in it? Not everyone can understand food labels — they're confusing at the best of times! My solution is to try to reduce food that comes out of a packet. Products that come in plastic can often be more processed and less healthy.

7. *Raw, whole foods*. On the other hand, eating food that is whole, raw and comes from nature is a great way to simplify what's best to eat. But as I've discussed, eating like this can be expensive and prohibitive. Whether or not you agree that the separate organic section at the supermarket is better for you, it's usually less affordable, so you have to work with your budget, and that's okay. Maybe there are one or two organic products you could buy one week, and then skip the pricey vegetable you could easily substitute. Another tip is to buy what's in season. It's cheaper and better quality because it hasn't had to sit in a freezer for months. You can research online to see what's good at particular times of the year.

My approach

As a kid, my eating habits were very strict. I never ate any junk food. If someone was eating a bag of chips and offered one to me, I would turn them down. Even though I knew one chip wasn't going to affect me, psychologically I thought I needed to have an edge on everyone else, and eating junk food wasn't going to give it to me.

Luckily, my mum always cooked healthy food, so it was easy to stay fuelled on what she made. There were sometimes sweets around the house, but I wouldn't eat them.

On the other hand, my dad is Lebanese, and my grandmother on his side was an amazing cook. We grew up with her cooking all this amazing Lebanese food at every family function and holiday. She taught a lot of the dishes to different family members before she died, and Dad became a really good a cook as a result.

When it comes to losing weight and getting fit, I think a lot of people don't realise what a dramatic difference good eating can make. Take this example: if an average-sized woman goes running for an hour, she'll burn about 450 calories. That's a little bit less than one Big Mac. The bottom line is that eating well is the easiest and most effective way to keep your weight under control, but you really must make time for the exercise, too.

Eating disorders

As I've mentioned, around the time I developed an addiction to exercise, I also developed incredibly unhealthy eating habits. This went hand in hand with my obsessive approach of pushing myself at all costs. In this case, I was fixated on training harder and doing more than anyone else. I wanted to know I could push myself beyond normal limits. The result was incredibly unhealthy behaviour.

In addition to training myself into the ground, I developed a severe eating disorder—something that I still to this day feel shame talking about. I slowly started eliminating foods from my diet as I felt a need to get an extra edge in any way possible. It went from not allowing myself to eat certain junk foods, to eliminating junk food, to eventually cutting food to the point of malnourishment. There was no logic in it as I knew that I needed nourishment to fuel myself for competing, but I simply couldn't control it. The compulsion was so strong. I would monitor everything that was put in front of me and would dread dinner time as I was always trying to work out how to avoid eating foods I found too fatty without upsetting Mum. Everyone around me could see it was an issue and was trying to help, but nothing would get through. The longer it went on, the worse it became. I remember looking back on photos from that time feeling horrified at how skinny I was. I looked malnourished and visibly unwell. This whole experience gave me a deeper understanding and empathy towards others who suffer from illnesses such as anorexia. It taught me that this can happen to anyone, no matter what mental health–related condition someone is experiencing.

Over time, I started making gradual changes, along with overcoming other issues. Because I hadn't worked on the fundamental, underlying problem, other issues, such as using alcohol to cope, kept coming up. The learning from this experience was that many problems manifest because of the underlying issues we often fail to address.

Any behaviour can become a problem if it becomes compulsive. And any behaviour can become compulsive. The mind starts to trick itself into believing that extreme behaviour is going to be somehow beneficial and make you feel safe and secure. In reality, it tears your life apart. The eating problem was one of the first encounters I had with compulsion on that level. It made no sense as I was an extremely fit and healthy young boy who in fact needed lots of sustenance to aid all the physical exertion, along with fuel for growth. I remember being aware of this but still not being able to change. I so badly wanted my body to develop and wanted to succeed as an athlete even more badly. Yet my compulsion was so strong that I just couldn't stop myself from limiting my diet.

It still upsets me to this day to think about and is something I have very rarely shared with people. I guess the learning here is that we all have things we're ashamed of. Yes, I've spent the past decade speaking about mental health education, my personal battles and how I overcame them, but I have rarely talked about the eating side of it. And writing about it here is helping to alleviate the shame I have felt.

Shame is one of the most horrible emotions we can feel. It comes with guilt, frustration, anger and leads to negative and unhealthy behaviour. As far as I have learned, the only way to start dealing with shame is to get honest and talk about it. If we bottle things up, they will fester, in the same way a plant will wilt or fruit will rot if not looked after. The problem will just become worse to the point of deeply affecting your wellbeing. I hope that by sharing this with you, and owning what I'm ashamed of, you might gain the strength to start talking about your problems, or encourage others to talk who have their own shame.

A final word

As with everything else in this book, we aren't talking about making crazy lifestyle changes. We're discussing simple and practical things that we can all do each day to take a small step forward. Most of us will be aware of the implications that a negative lifestyle can have, and the healthier options that are available, but will still fail to take action.

That's why it's important to experiment and play a little with what works for you, and then keep that up by doing it each day. That's what creates the habit, and that's what sets up the change in your brain to sustain longer term mental health.

There's a huge correlation between mental health and nutrition. Helping you feel good in your body will help you feel good in your mind. And good nutrition is vital to that connection.

Doing a little bit of the above, every day, over a long time, will make a big difference to your wellbeing.

Move Your Mind with Nick:
Make healthy changes to your diet

- *Explore different approaches.* There are many diets, supplements, and different trendy 'super foods' on the market, and it can all become confusing! Explore different approaches, and use self-awareness and common sense, as well as professional advice from your GP, to guide you.

- *Start thinking about your own health:*

  - Am I drinking more water than sugary or caffeinated drinks?

  - Am I drinking enough water to be fully hydrated?

  - Can I afford the requirements for the diet I am trying to follow? If not, what are the alternatives?

  - Am I eating out too often?

  - Am I eating at least one serve of a colourful vegetable with most meals, if not every meal?

  - Am I eating a palm-sized amount of animal or plant-based protein with every meal?

  - Do my ingredients come from sustainable and ethical producers?

  - Is what I'm eating heavily processed using chemicals and additives, or is it something that can grow by itself in nature? (Aim to eat the second option most often!)

- *Follow these simple tips:*

  - Eat at home more often.

(continued)

- Eat slowly—when you eat quickly, you trick yourself into eating more before your body responds to the food intake.

- Eat more fruit, vegetables and fresh foods.

- Avoid processed, fatty foods and sugars.

- Sleep more—lack of sleep has been shown to result in weight gain (more about this in chapter 8).

- Make yourself a smoothie every day for a week. Try a fruit and/or veggie smoothie—it's ultra-fast and delivers an excellent bunch of nutrients that will set you up for your day. Throw them in a blender, and you're done. While this is what works for me, it's going to be different for everybody. Test out some recipes, buy a blender and mix it up. If you buy a blender that you can simply tip over and drink from the mixer, there's less to clean up too!

I THINK WE HAVE BEEN TRAINED BY SOCIETY TO FLATTEN OUR EMOTIONS. IF SOMEONE SAYS, 'HOW ARE YOU?', WE OFTEN SAY, 'FINE ' ... WHICH TRANSLATES TO, 'F*CKED UP, INSECURE, NEUROTIC, AND EMOTIONALLY UNSTABLE'.

Malcolm Stern

CHAPTER 7

PATHWAY 3:
CONNECT YOUR MIND

As we move into the 21st century, we're experiencing a strange conundrum. We're more connected than ever before in human history, yet we couldn't be more disconnected. Technology has made the world a smaller place and has improved how we function in so many ways, but it's equally made us lazy and reliant. For example, we build a false sense of connection by gaining likes and validation on social media, sending text messages to a bunch of friends, and viewing other people's manicured display of their lives.

But all of this comes at the expense of something technology can never replace—face-to-face connection. Physical connection is a core human need we're missing out on more than ever. To live a well-rounded and healthy life, it's important that we find ways to connect our mind.

In this chapter, you're going to learn why there's such an issue globally around creating real connections. I'll share stories, expert opinions and strategies so you can see how to use technology in a healthy way and create daily habits to be better connected.

Key learnings

We all need healthy connections — and I don't mean ones based on technology.

1. *Mental diet:* When we talk about our diet we immediately think about food, but our diet extends to what we mentally consume too. Technology is a great example. It can be an amazing tool, but it can also be our downfall because of how constantly we are connected. From the moment we wake up until we fall asleep at night, we are connected to technology — often 24/7.

   You may have seen the documentary *The Social Dilemma*, which explores how technology companies are using humans as products they manipulate to improve their bottom lines. They design their platforms to be irresistible and highly addictive. Every time you get a new like, message or friend request, it releases a dopamine hit similar to the hit you receive when using recreational drugs. It's easy to get sucked in and impossible not to expect to become addicted, especially when you use social media daily. It's so intelligent, using machine learning to tailor content and the experience to your preferences, making it even harder to resist.

2. *Teens:* Teenagers are experiencing higher levels of stress than ever before, thanks to a number of factors: the fast-paced nature of life; the pressure to succeed academically, socially and athletically; increased exposure to media and screens; and a tendency to negatively compare themselves with the falsely idealised 'reality' provided by social media.

Platform use is currently unregulated for teens, even though, like alcohol and drugs, social media platforms manipulate brain chemistry and can become addictive. Screen time and social media usage are unprecedented for this age group, so the long-term consequences are yet to be identified.

3. *Cyberbullying:* Social bullying is extremely problematic in schools, and in extreme circumstances can lead to suicide. The Megan Meier Foundation states that 'approximately 34 per cent of students report experiencing cyberbullying during their lifetime' and that for more than 60 per cent of these student this 'significantly affected their ability to learn and feel safe while at school'.

The foundation also states that about 6 per cent of students have digitally self-harmed (that is, created an anonymous online account and cyberbullied themselves) and that students who experience cyberbullying are nearly twice as likely to attempt suicide.

This needs to change. Cyberbullying will not stop being a problem until extreme action is taken, whether it's government intervention in an ideal world, major regulation around these platforms and/or embedded education in schooling. Unfortunately, this is unlikely to happen any time soon because it takes so long to change systems. Yes, there is more awareness and yes, some schools are making more of a push, but stronger action is needed.

For a key change to happen in schools around the world, governments would need to create major agendas and rigid systems to ensure social media platforms and related mediums are monitored along with relevant education. Further to that, they would need strict protocols around these social media platforms to avoid their misuse. It's happening on a small level, but extreme change is unlikely any time soon.

(continued)

PATHWAY 3
CONNECT YOUR MIND

The good news is that you can learn how to take control yourself, which is what this book is all about. If you can create practices and educate yourself about using these platforms in a healthy way, you can pass these learnings on to your friends, or kids (if you are a parent). It would be unreasonable to ask you to stop using these platforms altogether—they are simply too embedded in society. Instead, learn to set a routine and structure around your usage and how and when you use technology. Look at what is positive and what has a negative impact on you and then set rigid structures around how and when you use it and stick to it.

A similar way of looking at this is through the lens of junk food. It's hard to eliminate junk food from your life; however, eating junk food all day, every day would be profoundly detrimental to your health. It's the same with technology. If you're on social media, listening to every opinion online and reading negative stories 24/7, it can drastically affect your mental health. Later in the chapter I will outline some strategies for putting this into practice.

4. *The power of real connection:* Some years ago, I was conducting a TEDx talk on the global suicide epidemic. It got me thinking about the power of connection. One of my statements was that one real conversation with a stranger, where you connect face to face, can be more powerful than having hundreds of Facebook friends or millions of Instagram followers. It's because connection is about being fully present and immersed in the situation at hand. I talked earlier about how unfulfilling it is when someone is distracted when you are with them.

Instead, lead by example. You need to remind yourself of this when you're guilty of being rude to others. When you make the effort not to be rude and offer your full attention, it makes you feel significantly better. The bottom line here is to work on being present and respectful in every interaction. No one person is more or less valuable than another. It doesn't matter what someone's wealth, status or social position is. We're all human, we all have emotions, we all must deal with ups and downs and we all deserve respect.

5. *Count your real friends on one hand:* I remember being told by a mentor how important it is to be able to count your close friends on one hand. Sure, it's great to know lots of people and have good people around you, but it's difficult to maintain more than five really close, unconditional friends. Like family, friendships take constant work from both ends—a real time commitment—and we only have so much time each day. But when you both put in the effort, it's amazing how much richness good, close friendships bring. They're friends you can really rely on, and friends you can lean on. I can't recall how many times I've leaned on my friends (and vice versa) over the years—they have been my lifeline. So, rather than trying to be the most popular person, or have the most social media followers, focus on creating quality and meaningful friendships that will be with you for life. You'll be thankful for it!

6. *You're a product of the top five people you spend your time with:* You may have heard this famous saying. It's from motivational speaker Jim Rohn, who said we're the average of the five people we spend the most time with. It's all to do with the law of averages, which is the theory that the result of any situation is the average of all outcomes.

If you adopt this thinking, who you spend your time with is critical, and you only have so much time each day. If you're surrounded by toxic, negative people, you'll naturally become more negative and begin to lose confidence and belief in yourself. But if you're around more positive people, you'll become more positive. And if you're around people who support and encourage you, your self-esteem will grow. It's important you're aware of this and use the opportunity to constantly assess the people you surround yourself

(continued)

with. You need to have the tools to deal with or walk away from negative relationships, and service the positive ones. Working on this will most definitely change your life for the better.

7. *Self-love:* Self-love is particularly important. It's hard to connect with and be loving to others if you don't have love for yourself. This isn't something you can achieve overnight, either. It takes daily work and a lot of soul searching, but it's one of the most important things you can do for yourself. This book has many examples of how to improve self-love, from taking time out for yourself, looking after your overall wellness through eating well, exercising and meditating, and seeing a therapist, to simply doing the things you love. I want this book to guide you to work on yourself. We can't truly love others until we can learn to love ourselves.

8. *Quality over quantity:* I often hear people say they can't connect in the way they need to because they don't have a close family or enough available friends. On the other hand, there are many people who are around family and friends 24/7 yet don't receive the connection they crave. It comes down to quality versus quantity.

   Doing one kind-hearted and selfless act for someone in need is more powerful than making 100 million dollars for your own personal gain. Get your priorities right, simplify things and focus on what's truly important. This is something available to all of us, and not just reserved for the elite few. Later in this chapter, I'll explore this in more detail, and look at lessons learned from people in their dying days.

9. *It's all connected!* When it comes to wellness and mental wellbeing, everything is connected. If you want to become more connected, you need to become a better listener. If you want to become a better listener, you need to become more present. If you want to become more present, you need to practise things like meditation, self-love and patience.

INSIGHTS FROM MALCOLM STERN

Malcolm Stern is a psychotherapist, executive coach, author and television presenter with 30 years' international experience. I met Malcolm when I interviewed him for the Move Your Mind *podcast. Despite being in his 70s, we instantly connected and chatted well beyond the interview. He's one of the most accomplished and experienced mental health professionals in the UK and I knew I had to include his wisdom in the book!*

How much do we really care about each other? I think we have been trained by society to flatten our emotions. If someone says, 'How are you?', we often say, 'Fine', which translates to 'F*cked up, insecure, neurotic and emotionally unstable'. Instead, I think there's a real need for us to have genuine communication and connection with others. That is our salvation in the sense of feeling part of a tribe—ultimately, the family of humanity.

As technology advances, we have also lost that tribal village-like connection. We can have thousands of Facebook friends, but not recognise 90 per cent of them. Social media can be like an echo chamber too—I don't want to be reading from people who agree with me all the time. Then, there's the other side of those who violently disagree with you and knock everything you say.

Instead, you just need four or five friends you can count on one hand and talk to about your life, your purpose and other things, rather than your philosophies and political beliefs. Ask questions like, 'Who are you? What's your essence? What's your role in the world? Who do you strive to become in the world?' It comes back to finding your own tribe. I have a weekly, one-hour catch-up with a friend where we spend 20 minutes each talking, and 10 minutes reflecting without interrupting each other. It's important to get a real reflection of how we are showing up with others who genuinely care about us and connect with us.

(continued)

I also think taking in so much information from technology, media and social media is overloading our brains and sort of dehumanising us. Since moving to the country, I have found it very important to spend time in nature away from technology. The respite from consuming information is essential, but it's so easy to get caught up in it. I want to nourish myself through meditation, nature and time away from distraction, so I make it a discipline of swimming against the current because the tide is trying to bring us noise in the form of news, media, and so on.

For example, I had a woman come and see me who was addicted to watching programs on television. I introduced her to meditation and it has changed her life. Not only has her mood improved and she's no longer caught up in the habit, but also her relationships with her children have improved. We get the reflections from the mirror around us: the people we have relationships with.

Finally, I think external things can give you a buzz and you may feel really high for a while, but ultimately, the only thing that brings peace and connection to your depth of self is the work you do on yourself. I don't think you can ever get that from external forces. In fact, all the mystics and wise people who came before us have said the same thing. I'm not really saying anything too new. There have been studies done that, beyond a certain level of income, there's no difference in happiness levels. Whether you're earning $10 million a year or $50 000 a year, once you're past the survival mechanism and you're no longer worried about putting food in your mouth or a roof over your head, then your wellbeing comes from within. I think people who have a lot of material possessions almost feel obliged to show how fantastic it all is. But we need to be alone by ourselves as well.

For me, the quality of connection is the meaning of life. And it's essential to gather your community. Until we reach a certain stage in our evolution, not only do we have a need for support of others of like mind, but we also have a duty to seek that support. Evolution is happening; it's just that it's three steps forwards, two steps backwards. I think we are becoming what we can become, which is something far bigger than what we are right now.

Move Your Mind with Malcolm: Be present and authentic

- *Bear witness:* Next time you find yourself with someone who is unhappy or angry, practise bearing witness to them. Don't judge or try to find solutions.

  Rather than sympathise, notice what is happening inside you as you do this. Often when we feel disturbed, our breathing quickens, and in slowing it down we give ourselves an extra resource. Let yourself make contact with your bodily sensations as you continue relating. Become aware of your own breathing and your ability to maintain eye contact. In holding the gaze of another you are letting them know and reassuring them that what they are saying isn't overwhelming. If you catch yourself avoiding eye contact, be honest with yourself: is it too much for you? If so, be straight with the other person and find a compassionate way of saying, 'I can't do this'.

  In this practice you will discover a deep capacity and interest in other human beings. But there are no quick fixes. You're retraining yourself to be authentic with others, and as you pursue this you will notice when you are truly bearing witness and when you are pretending. Don't judge yourself, but when you notice your lack of presence, draw your attention back, either by eye contact and breathing, or by honest communication.

  Observe your propensity for switching off (we do it a lot) and make a conscious choice to bring your attention to what's happening in front of you. Flex this muscle and you will find that it will do it itself after a while.

(continued)

PATHWAY 3
CONNECT YOUR MIND

Expand this practice into everyday life. When you walk past trees, observe their differences and their beauty. When you get on the train, refrain from using your phone and going into your own world. Let yourself be someone who drinks in the environment around you. You don't have to do it 24 hours a day—just enough to stretch this muscle. A by-product of this is that you will be far more adept and enjoyable to be with in a relationship. We are goal-oriented animals, and if you find yourself achieving some success it gives you great motivation to continue the practice.

• *Invest in your like-minded community:* Commit to the practice of connecting with depth and get conscious about your relationships.

– Where do you feel heart connection?

– Where can you be honest?

– With whom can you be vulnerable?

Decide who in your life you want to invest in, and where there is a call to expand your circle of friends. See if you can go deeper with the relationships you want to nurture. When you meet people who are important to you, make sure you talk about what really matters rather than just passing the time. Be willing to release your mask of being 'fine' and be daring in your willingness to communicate in a more authentic way.

Could you find one other person who is on your wavelength and who you feel supported by and supportive of? Suggest formalising that relationship so there is dedicated time given to building a place of depth between you.

If you're psychologically minded, then perhaps a therapy group, or men's and women's groups, may work for you. If you're creatively minded, maybe you could join an amateur dramatics association, or a pottery, writing or painting group. If you're a physical, hands-on person, a walking and running group could be for you. If you're spiritually minded, a meditation or yoga group could work. When I was at yoga recently my teacher acknowledged what a gift it was to be able to do the practice with so many like-minded others, and I did indeed feel enriched.

Love and connection

I'm fortunate to have an incredibly close extended family with relationships I will cherish forever. The difficult thing that comes with that is dealing with death. I was speaking to a mental health expert recently about this and she made a truly remarkable comment: 'The price we pay for loving so deeply is the pain that follows. Many people don't get to experience such pain, but they also miss out on the amazing experience of having deep, loving relationships'.

I had a very close relationship with my Uncle Bruce and Aunty Rob (Bruce's wife and my dad's sister). They were two of the most important people in my life, with Bruce mentoring me and believing in me since I was a little kid (as I shared in Chapter 5) and Rob being there for me emotionally as I got older. They were my rock and I knew that wherever I was in the world, or whatever I was facing, I could handle it because I had them in my corner. They were the two most incredible people you could ever meet. Bruce was unique, eccentric and unapologetically himself, and Rob was the most caring, selfless person I have met to this day.

During the pandemic, Bruce was moved to a nursing home due to his motor neurone disease worsening. He had held on for 10 years when doctors had given him only two, with Rob sacrificing her life to care for him on her own, despite being urged to get support. While

Bruce's condition was deteriorating, Rob was diagnosed with lung cancer. It came out of the blue and was a shock because—even though she was in her early 70s—she was incredibly energetic, vibrant and healthy. Her health worsened rapidly and led to a really tough period.

When Bruce passed away, Rob's lung cancer was progressing and no chemotherapy or treatment was working. It all happened so fast and she passed away just a few weeks after Bruce. It was a whirlwind of a time and something that will stick with me for the rest of my life. I'm thankful to have had the opportunity to be there for them and to see them regularly during those final months.

I learnt so much from my relationship with Rob and Bruce even during that very painful time. I saw what it meant to be selfless and to care unconditionally. I learnt lessons from them such as never putting things off, following your heart and living life to the full. It really engrained in me that we only have one shot at life, only so much time on the planet, and that there is no use in wasting it or putting anything off. It has been incredibly difficult no longer having them in my corner but every time I doubt myself or face a difficult challenge, I think of Rob and Bruce and push myself to do it for them because I know it would make them proud.

It's impossible to love people and have these kinds of relationships without having to deal with pain at some point, but I wouldn't trade it for the world. Rob and Bruce changed my life forever and I now live by the mantra of following my heart and dreams with them always in mind. I hope others can be as lucky as I have been and have similar relationships in their lives … nothing is more important than having that kind of connection.

Fortunately, I've only had a handful of experiences of being around a loved one in their dying days. Each time I've experienced it, I've asked them what they found most important in life. Almost every time, it was being around those they loved and simply doing and saying the things they wanted.

Australian nurse Bronnie Ware found a similar pattern. She wrote a blog and a book of her patients' dying words as she looked after them during palliative care.

The top five regrets that they expressed to her were that:

1. they wished they had had the courage to live a life true to themselves, not a life others expected of them

2. they wished they hadn't worked so hard

3. they wished they had had the courage to express their feelings

4. they wished they had stayed in touch with their friends

5. they wished they had let themselves be happier.

From everything I've learned, read and experienced, it all comes down to love and connection. What's life without it? Why do people work so hard to make more money, buy the biggest house and have the most perfect family? Why do people slave away at jobs they hate? Why do people put on a front and try to be someone they're not? Does this bring happiness? I've met people all over the world who make hundreds of millions of dollars but aren't happy. Are they trying to gain something we all inherently want? Are they trying to trying to use money as a means to buy happiness and connection?

When it comes to connection, everything comes at a price. Everything you do will have positive and negative implications, so it's important to decide what is worth suffering for. Love and connection, in my opinion, are worth suffering for. There's no feeling better than unconditional love and you can't find that without allowing yourself to be vulnerable.

We're social creatures, and our need for social connection is fundamental to our being. Creating those core social connections doesn't have to be hard. Everything you need and want is available to you now if you're willing to be open and vulnerable enough to embrace it. We try so hard to impress others and be someone else, but love can't be gained, bought, stolen or found by being someone we're not. Love comes from being your true self, showing vulnerability and being authentic. It comes from helping people, which also has the by-product of leaving you feeling amazing. If you can live like this, the people who are meant to be in your life will naturally be there. If you can grasp this, your life can be so much easier to manage.

Connection comes from within

Researchers agree that the benefits of connection are linked to your personal sense of connection. So, if you feel connected to others on the inside, you'll reap the benefits. It just takes a bit of spirit and sense of adventure.

You can put yourself out there, do your best and have the best intentions, but often things don't go your way—whether it's friendships, your financial situation, work life or something else. Think about it in the same way as you look at your physical health: you can't control getting sick or having an illness. But you can control what you eat, how much you sleep, when you exercise and so on.

It's the same for your mind. You control how you choose to react and what you choose to learn from situations. You can work on yourself from within and make your best efforts to create a rich inner world and stable mental state with daily tasks such as meditation, gratitude journalling, connecting with people and challenging yourself, for example, which are all tools I address in this book. In doing so, you'll be less affected by external events, and more likely to thrive inside and out.

INSIGHTS FROM KARIN BLAK

Karin Blak is a UK-based psychosexual and relationship therapist, qualified couples counsellor and author of **The Essential Companion to Talking Therapy.** *I interviewed Karin on my* **Move Your Mind** *podcast and went straight back to her when I needed an expert for the relationship section of this book, as she is at the top of her field.*

How healthy you are psychologically will inform how you act in your relationships. One of the most important things you can do when you interact with others is to be aware of what you're doing yourself. If you can be aware of this rather than try to analyse the person you're speaking with—your partner—you stand a better chance of a balanced interaction. We can often act out on our partner in anger when our past is triggered, and this can be avoided with more self-awareness. This is so important in everyday interactions, especially relationships, and it's vital to continue developing your skills, self-development and self-awareness so that you know what's going on in your body better.

However, you don't need to have everything sorted to be in a relationship. Can you imagine having a relationship with no space for issues? That would be dreadful, wouldn't it? If you had a partner who thought they were perfect, and expected the same of you, and one day you're really struggling to get through the day, how would they cope with you struggling? Throw in a pandemic, and there are even more pressures on modern relationships. In fact, COVID-19 has led to more marriage breakdowns over the traditional statistic of one in four marriages ending in divorce.

If your expectations are so high, the only way you can have a relationship is if it's perfect 100 per cent of the time. And that's just not possible. You're going to let yourself down, your partner

(continued)

down and you're always going to be disappointed. There will always be challenges in life, so you shouldn't take them out on your partner. There needs to be balance and acceptance of imperfections on both ends, so it's important you learn to understand each other and learn about their needs and what triggers them. How will you manage things in the relationship when your buttons are triggered? By sticking by them and working through things.

A great analogy I like to use is that the relationship becomes more like a room you go in and out of. You might carry a piece of it in your pocket, preferably the piece that says 'I'm loved, I belong'. You can come out of that and have a life outside, go to work, go to your hobby and come back into the relationship and share and belong and love and do all this kind of stuff — but that's not possible initially because you don't know each other well enough.

One person in our lives is not enough. You need more than one person, and again it's about being self-aware. You need this hole to be filled, so do you fill it with chocolates, alcohol or a person or do you sit down and look at what is going on with you?

I also believe we have different relationships that mean different things at different times in life. For example, a teenage relationship is unlikely to last. There is also a view that some relationships serve a stage in our lives while working through things. For example, a relationship may work while you have kids but not work so well after they grow up and leave home.

Ultimately, I think instead of looking too far ahead and aiming for a relationship to last forever, you should just focus on the here and now. Nurture what you have. Personally, I've learned this firsthand. I wasn't very good at relationships before I became a therapist. I certainly know during my first marriage that I married for all the wrong reasons and because of pressure from my parents as it was a marriage that would give me status. Of course, it didn't work because my heart wasn't in it. Everyone needs to find their own unique path.

Furthermore, relationships change over time. Usually, one person grows and then the partner catches up and vice versa. As long as the growth is in small increments and you can catch up with each other, then the relationship will be okay. If one person goes to therapy or does a big piece of self-development, the partner really needs to do something as well so they can work together — so they are balanced in self-development. I've worked with quite a few couples where that didn't happen, and some weren't able to realise that they needed to develop as well, and as a result those relationships didn't last.

Move Your Mind with Karin: Spend time together

In your intimate relationships, the most important thing you can do is spend time together. It doesn't matter what you do, as long as it's together, so think of fun, shared experiences to nurture and engage with each other in different ways. For example:

* *have a games night*: anything from computer or online games to board games like Monopoly or Scrabble

* *enjoy a music night*: as you've already read in this book, listening to music is a great way to reduce stress. But it's also ideal for a long-term relationship because reminiscing with music is great for reflection and your history and can be what keeps couples together

* *organise a movie night*: grab some popcorn and a choc top and get out and see a new film. Or stay at home and do it for free — movies offer a great experience

* *get out into nature*: going on regular walks in a park nearby or in the countryside is both healing and free of charge. It can include as many or as few people as you want too.

PATHWAY 3
CONNECT YOUR MIND

My approach

I took a gap year after finishing high school, which is where you take a break for 12 months before starting university. I thought it would be a good opportunity to move out of my comfort zone to the UK, as I didn't feel ready for university. It turned out to be one of the most difficult things I've ever done.

At the age of 18, I was so shy I couldn't hold a one-on-one conversation with anyone, and was terrified of eye contact. I had not learned to interact with others and was afraid of expressing myself.

But I got on the plane and flew overseas to a school called Marlborough College, near Bath and Bristol, about three hours from London. As part of the gap year, I was required to help out as a teacher's aide with sporting activities.

With a background as an athlete in track and field, I would attend the nightly track sessions and then go to the physical education classes during the day.

I found some relief being at the athletics track, but due to my insecurities and shyness, I had no confidence and felt completely out of my depth having to tell other students what to do. I was terrified to meet new people and come out of my shell, despite the best efforts of other student teachers to connect with me. I gradually withdrew mentally and physically, spending weeks on end by myself.

The school's prestige meant that the catered daily meals were sensational, and my routine became sleeping in until midday, sitting alone in the lunch area eating three to four serves of whatever had been made, then watching *Neighbours*, ironically a show I would end up on, before a walk or jog through the forest on the edge of the town. Another three to four helpings of dinner was next, timed while everyone had just finished so I could eat alone, followed by strolling home and buying two large packets of chips, which I'd eat while watching two movies—one packet per film—until 3 am. And repeat.

It was the only time in my adult life I've been so blasé about exercise while over-indulging in food, but it was how I coped with the mental health struggles I faced. I lived like this for almost a year, interspersed with visits to my best friend, Huw, the same friend who was in the car crash with me a few years later. He was living in Wolverhampton doing his gap year, and we would catch up and travel around Europe whenever we could.

Crippled by insecurity at the college, it was a different story when travelling. I had the opportunity to abuse alcohol more and I used the loss of my inhibitions to compensate for everything else that was wrong in my life. Like much of my early 20s, I was completely out of control, with drinking the only way I could break out of my shell and connect with others. It was such an extreme contrast to my isolated bubble at the college, and now that I look back I genuinely feel lucky to have gotten through it.

As I outlined in chapter 1, I was afraid of my own shadow, confused and didn't know what to do. Drinking was the only way I could find temporary calmness. If I'd been informed in the same way that I hope this book will hopefully inform you, I may have been able to seek help earlier, realise I was not alone and make better decisions.

That's why I'm so motivated to help people and inform and educate others. We're quick to label people as broken or troubled before taking the time to see what is really going on.

I also want to note how lucky I am to have amazing parents. We haven't always seen eye to eye, but their support has been unconditional and they have been there for me every step of the way. I feel so lucky. In fact, it was my dad's running for a third term as premier of Victoria that put an end to my UK gap year. I was supposed to be there until year's end, but his election was in November and I didn't want to miss it so I came back early.

Relationships

For many years, I lacked intimate relationships in my life. I was too afraid to let people in and always fed myself the narrative that there was something better out there. The reality was the huge fear I had built up through my adolescence that I wasn't good enough. I felt that way through the trauma of not developing, of not fitting in and not having the confidence to be myself.

Rather than acknowledge this, I allowed it to go on for many years. I relied on alcohol to get close to people and would push them away as soon as they became interested. I had commitment issues and used every excuse I could to avoid anyone getting close to me. I was too scared to be intimate with a girl unless I was drunk and denied myself so many experiences.

It wasn't until I finally forced myself to confront it in my late 20s that I ended up in the first relationship of my life. It was an experience I had so desperately wanted and I was overwhelmed by the feelings that came with it. It was exciting and terrifying at the same time. After two years, it ended in heartbreak, another first experience for me. I was in agony at the time and spent 12 months struggling to simply make it through each day. I thought I would never recover.

Now, looking back, I'm so glad that it happened. The relationship made me grow and learn, while having my heart broken forced me to confront some of my deepest fears. I wanted to feel every single bit of the pain and learn and understand my faults and why they are there. It was the best thing that could have happened to me and I am grateful to this day for the learnings that came from it.

A final word

In short, we all need connection. It's part of our fabric, brings us together and makes us grow. As technology and the world evolve, things are becoming much more complicated and are threatening to take this away from us. It's an irony of life and can be summed up in the saying, 'be careful what you wish for'. The best and worst thing about humanity is our drive for more. It creates opportunity and advances us as a society, but ultimately comes at a cost.

In life, things will always change and evolve. You need to learn to adapt, make the most of the good and learn from the bad. You can't ignore what's going on in the world and how it functions, so instead you must learn to look after yourself while participating in it. I really hope that the following section on changing your mindset enlightens you on connecting your mind and leaves you with some simple and sustainable tools you can start practising daily.

Move Your Mind with Nick:
Change your mindset

- *Leave your phone at home.* Next time you're going out for dinner or lunch with a friend or family member, leave your phone behind. If that sounds too hard, try a shorter time period by having a coffee instead of a meal. What I want you to focus on is how it makes you feel with your phone at home. Weird? Naked? Incomplete? Or maybe more connected with the person you're with? You may feel uncomfortable about it initially, but hopefully over time you'll do it more and more and it'll become a good habit. We'll talk more about habits in part IV.

- *Halve your screen time for 21 days.* Cutting down device usage isn't easy. Don't be too hard on yourself if you struggle to put the phone or tablet down. If you accidentally forget your commitment and binge an entire season of your favourite television show over the weekend, that's okay. Any progress is progress — take the challenge one day at a time, log your progress as you go and if you miss a day, just pick up from where you left off!

I THINK THE MOST IMPORTANT THINGS WE CAN LEARN ARE THE ABILITY TO BE PRESENT, PAY ATTENTION, LIVE CONSCIOUSLY AND LEARN THE NUANCE TO CALM THE MIND.

Dr Craig Hassed

CHAPTER 8

PATHWAY 4:
STILL YOUR MIND

Meditation, mindfulness and sleep are three key ingredients when it comes to mental health and wellbeing. In recent times, they've become buzz words, with thousands of books, apps, videos and programs covering it all. Like everything in this book, I want to make things easy, so I'll provide real stories, information and simple tools to put in place without overwhelming you.

I'm going to explore a range of real-life examples of mindfulness and meditation, dive into some short stories and look at different techniques of mindfulness practice. I'll also discuss sleep: why it's so important and how you can create better sleep patterns. Finally, I'll cover why this is a global issue and ways for you to incorporate meditation and mindfulness into your daily life.

Key learnings

Mindfulness and meditation are incredibly powerful. Don't listen to the naysayers—give them a go using the following tips and find out for yourself just how life-changing they can be.

1. *Find a style that works for you.* Many people think meditation is a weird spiritual thing when it's actually scientific. At its core, it's about training your brain to focus on one thing at a time. Remember this because that's basically all there is to it.

   It's not an outcome-based practice either. There's no 'good' or 'bad' meditation and it's okay if you don't feel 'Zen' the entire time. The key is the repeated process of returning your attention to one idea.

   Luckily, there are many ways to meditate, which means it's easy to find a style that works for you. There's no need to sit cross-legged and chant 'Om' if you don't enjoy it. You don't have to sit on a remote mountain, shave your head and disappear for 20 years to reap the benefits either.

   Practising meditation can be as simple as sitting comfortably in a quiet place and bringing your attention to something uninteresting, like your breathing or the sound of an air conditioner. As you naturally become distracted by your thoughts, you return your attention to your breath once more. You'll know it's right if the process feels comfortable and effortless.

2. *Download an app.* Using an app like Headspace makes it easy for busy people to experience the cumulative benefits of a little meditation every day. Start small, practising for only a few minutes at a time, before building up to an extended meditation as you become comfortable with the technique. Feelings of boredom and overwhelm have incorrectly convinced people that meditation doesn't work

or isn't for them. Starting small and gradually building up means you can avoid this trap.

3. *Change is good.* Reaching rock bottom is a great thing. When you've run out of answers, you're more likely to try something completely new and crazy to solve your problems. It's a great time to open your mind to alternative ways of thinking and learn some new skills. You're conditioned to fear change when the reality is that change is good and very healthy. By trying different techniques, behaviours and habits, you'll certainly come across things that don't work for you, but it'll also lead you closer towards things that will. Look at it as a positive and something exciting as you open up a world of possibilities!

4. *Scientifically proven benefits.* Meditation is like a gym for the mind and research shows there are many proven health benefits of regular meditation. For example, the 'fear' processing part of the brain — the amygdala — shrinks after each meditation practice. The cortical lining of the hippocampus — the manager of memory and learning — thickens. Meditation is not only proven to be more restful than sleep, but is also shown to boost energy, mental health, performance and effectiveness. The best part is that meditation is a free and natural way to dramatically improve your mental wellbeing. The more you practise and reap the benefits, the more likely you'll never look back. It can be truly life changing.

5. *Don't judge your thoughts.* Mindfulness is especially helpful to manage ideas that are self-critical, anxious, pessimistic or overwhelming without reacting to them. This is because practising mindfulness means allowing thoughts to come and go without automatically investing in them. The average person has more than 6000 thoughts per day — good, bad and indifferent. It's a lot of thinking to process, and it's impossible to give equal weight to it all. While you

(continued)

can't control what you think about, you do have the ability to decide what you give power to.

Does the following sound familiar? You try to push away a negative thought, only for it to have the adverse effect and grow stronger in your mind. Or, you tell yourself a negative story, such as, 'I'm not good enough' because of a negative experience you had as a kid. Rather than try to stop the thoughts, try to acknowledge them, understand where they're coming from and remind yourself they're simply not true. Remind yourself that thoughts are only stories that you tell yourself — try not to give power to them.

This is all about the power of self-awareness. Whenever a negative thought comes up, embrace the negative emotion, accept the discomfort, remind yourself that it's not true and continue on with whatever you were doing.

6. *Become comfortable with the uncomfortable.* Meditation and mindfulness techniques increase your ability to tolerate discomfort. You'll be able to 'sit' with uncomfortable thoughts and high-pressure situations without taking undesirable action as a response to stress. It's a technique that will become invaluable in daily life. Rather than being reactive, you can learn to accept and understand the emotion you're feeling.

   Road rage is a good example most of us can relate to. Most people have either been on the receiving end or experienced it themselves. When it happens, rather than react, accept the uncomfortable emotion and understand that the rage is likely part of a bigger frustration. Look at it as a sign to work on yourself.

7. *Manage anxiety and depression.* Anxiety and depression stem from worrying about the past or future, which immobilises your ability to take necessary, helpful action

in the present moment. On the other hand, mindfulness allows you to be present and restfully alert in the current moment, as opposed to being on autopilot for more extended periods throughout the day. One hundred per cent presence is not achievable on a regular basis, but you can improve your mood and effectiveness with incremental bouts of mindfulness every day.

8. *Focus on what you can control.* The world can be so demanding, and you can put so much pressure on yourself that you get stuck trying to control every situation. Rather than worry about an uncontrollable situation, instead focus on what you can influence. Remind yourself regularly there's no point in worrying about things you can't control and redirect that energy into things you can. A lot of this involves using common sense and logic. But, as they say, 'common sense is not that common'. Mental energy spent worrying over an uncontrollable factor will not change your experience of that factor for the better.

9. *Use media to your advantage.* Mindfully pay attention to media content that helps you, not media that wastes your time or makes you feel bad after consuming it. Focus on material that inspires, educates and motivates you towards your daily purpose. It doesn't mean you can't enjoy a funny cat video here and there when you need a quick break. But if you keep the majority of your time and attention on media that helps you to grow, you'll be more likely to be satisfied with yourself at the end of the day. As we've already seen, you need to set boundaries around your content consumption. Like most things, too much is not a good thing.

10. *Embrace empathy.* One of the most powerful ways to become more mindful and appreciative of life is through empathy. You may often feel like you're alone in your suffering or get so caught up in your own problems that you take them out of context and lose touch with reality.

(continued)

PATHWAY 4
STILL YOUR MIND

But every single person in the world has a set of unique challenges they face. It doesn't matter who you are.

Taking some time to think about this, placing yourself in other people's shoes and also genuinely listening to other people's struggles will make a world of difference to your own life. Obviously, there are problems that need to be addressed — your health, the health of others, finances, and so on. But you can also find yourself getting caught up in creating problems that aren't a big deal in the overall scheme of things. Embracing empathy will help put this in context.

11. *Keep sleep regular.* It's really important to keep a routine when it comes to sleep, even on weekends. This can be a pain and may feel as though it takes away the spontaneity of life, but it can help you achieve sustained sleep. If you regularly mix up the time you go to bed and when you get up, you will confuse your body clock and this will result in less restful sleep. Commit to daily habits such as exercise, not taking naps (or at least not napping longer than 20 minutes), avoiding alcohol and caffeine later in the day, and not eating a heavy meal before bed.

12. *Mindfulness and sleep.* Mindfulness can be incredibly effective when it comes to sleep. It's often not until you're lying down at night, away from the distractions of the day, that you start to worry about life. Unsurprisingly, this can be incredibly destructive to your sleep. Mindfulness can help create the mental space needed to calm your mind and drift off to sleep.

What's more, it can help you to become more accepting and less stressed about sleep. Like anything relating to the mind, if you try to fight against it, the problem will only become worse. If you lie in bed stressing about whether or not you'll get enough sleep, it can really become a problem. I found this out the hard way, as you'll soon read. If you're struggling to sleep and feel anxious, accept it, practise some of the mindfulness techniques in this chapter and trust you will be okay.

I can't emphasise enough the importance of mindfulness for every person in our fast-paced world, so I've called on a mindfulness expert to provide more evidence of the value it can add to our lives.

INSIGHTS FROM DR CRAIG HASSED

Dr Craig Hassed OAM is an internationally renowned expert on mindfulness, and a pioneer of the use of mindfulness meditation within the medical world as a published author, GP and associate professor. I met Craig a few years ago after reaching out to him to contribute on a mindfulness project. We've stayed in touch ever since and he's always been generous in lending his time. I wanted his insight as he is one of the leading mindfulness experts in the world, having explored the subject since the 1980s from a scientific standpoint.

In 2020, there were about 2000 papers on mindfulness published in peer review journals. That's around five or six a day! The research shows that it's getting harder than ever to find balance in the modern world because we're constantly distracted through the misuse of technology, social media and screen time.

One peer-reviewed article showed how cognitive processes and attention circuits in the brain are changing due to overuse of the online world. If you think about your own computer use, it's not uncommon to have 20 tabs open, constant pings and other stuff going off — our attention is all over the place. Worse still, our memory is wasting away because we now use our phones instead of our brains. Social and emotional intelligence is also suffering because we have our faces buried in our phones rather than interacting face to face with others.

Furthermore, a significant concern is that at least one-third, and in some countries possibly 40 per cent, of young people have

(continued)

PATHWAY 4
STILL YOUR MIND

a diagnosable addiction to their devices. Like an addiction to a drug, the device starts to replace other things like work and self-care, which the person can't control, until it begins to dominate their life and their attention.

Short of educating parents and teachers, we need to teach our children healthy habits, like using technology wisely from an early age. Around the world, some governments are taking steps to not allow smartphones in class. Hopefully this can be taken on broadly. It's a great step forward as it doesn't demonise technology but shows kids how to set reasonable limits.

My opinion is that we need mindfulness now more than ever. Mindfulness helps with stress, anxiety and depression by improving performance, memory, communication, decision making, executive function, better immunity and resistance to disease. It also slows the ageing process and takes stress away from the cardiovascular system. Medically, people coping with serious illness or dealing with chronic pain who practise mindfulness can cope better. Physically, mindfulness and meditation can dramatically help with staying in the zone for sports and performance. It also helps with emotional intelligence and relationships. After all, these are the important things that glue society together.

I believe we need to understand how to be present, pay attention, live consciously and learn the nuance of calming the mind. This isn't always easy — the more we try, the more frustrating it is. But we can learn not to be disturbed by the mind by standing back and not getting caught in the negative thought patterns.

Think of it like being on a train station platform. Trains of thought are coming and going, but you're not being moved by the trains. You can't force your mind to stop thinking, but if you can learn not to be reactive, you can instead accept the thinking, observe and choose not to react. Eventually, you'll allow your mind to settle itself.

I also like the analogy of a busy marketplace. Somebody comes up to you and tries to sell you things, and while you can't stop them, you can show them you're disinterested, and eventually they'll stop hassling you. Our minds are a little bit like that. They go on and on about this and that, but if you're not interested, in its own time, your mind will be quiet by itself.

This sense of quietness, resilience and inner peace is also closely related to ideas of happiness. We have this view that happiness comes from material things, and we are always getting things and having things, which are all outside of ourselves. In doing so, we try to avoid everything that is uncomfortable, which doesn't lead to a resilient self. It's only when we learn not to attach to things, or to let go of them, that we find inner peace.

So, your priority should be to do things that are meaningful. If you have a greater sense of meaning, you're more likely to be able to cope with something that's uncomfortable — because it's meaningful to you. You might find reading this book isn't comfortable, easy or pleasant at times, and that it's pretty hard work. But you're enduring the challenge and discomfort because it's meaningful to you!

Move Your Mind with Craig: Practise meditation

- Carve out some time to practise mindfulness meditation at least once every day.

- Practise savouring life and being present even during the mundane moments.

- Be curious and open to the possibility of learning from every life experience.

Scientific benefits of meditation and mindfulness

As we've already seen, meditation and mindfulness have fantastic benefits. They help to bring awareness away from the past and future, and into the present, and, in doing so, boost mental health, mood and performance while reducing stress, anxiety and depression — all as the brain works more effectively.

There have been thousands of studies performed on meditation and mindfulness and the results have been very positive, often showing them to be in many cases (like exercise) as effective as antidepressants. For example, a University of Oxford study found that mindfulness-based cognitive therapy (MBCT) is just as effective as antidepressants for preventing a relapse of depression, something that affects 50–80 per cent of people after their first bout.

I'm not saying that antidepressants, therapy and medication aren't important—they're often critical—but when it comes to mental health, there are so many options available worth investigating. The benefits of mindfulness and meditation is that they are predominantly free and completely self-sustainable.

Here are just a few of their benefits.

- By practising mindfulness and meditation every day, decluttering your mind and de-stressing yourself, you can literally add years to your life.

- Mindfulness and meditation calm the mind and allow creativity and problem solving. Having a clear mind can help you perform better by giving you more clarity and control.

- Being more mindful helps you to better understand yourself and others, ultimately leading to better relationships.

- Stress can lead to extreme health problems, including in some cases heart attacks. Meditation and mindfulness help to manage and prevent the onset of stress and to build the skills to manage stress more effectively.

- They bring about a deep sense of relaxation not only during the practice but for the whole day.

- They can reduce anxiety, depression, sleep problems and headaches, although they're not a replacement for traditional medical treatment.

Ways to meditate

There are a variety of techniques and approaches to suit anyone looking to meditate. Plus, it's easy to get started—look online or download an app. And you only need to do a small amount every day.

Techniques include:

- *guided meditation*. This focuses on guided imagery or visualisation.

- *mantra meditation*. This is where you repeat a calming word.

- *mindfulness meditation*. This focuses on the flow of your breath, as we explored at the start of this chapter.

- *qi gong*. This is a branch of traditional Chinese medicine focused on meditation, relaxation, physical movement and breathing exercises.

- *tai chi*. This is a gentle form of Chinese martial arts.

- *transcendental meditation*. This is my favourite, and I'll delve into it more later in the chapter.

- *yoga*. This is about moving through a series of postures and controlled breathing exercises.

Make it work for you

I have created daily habits including exercise and meditation that I do no matter what, whether I'm feeling good or bad. They are practices that keep me grounded and feeling healthy and clear, no matter what's happening around me.

Furthermore, it's not just about creating these habits so you can cope when things become bad. It's doing them rain, hail or shine. When things are good and you're looking after yourself, you can use them to get that bit more out of your day. When you've lost motivation, they can spark you into action. And when you're feeling down or losing hope, they can become your crutch.

I can't recall how many times I've drawn on my daily habits — they are my wellness tools. When I had periods where my work and social life felt like they were falling apart, I would use my daily habits to gain comfort in the fact that I could still control something, make myself feel good and gain a little peace of mind despite everything.

Here's your chance to create your own, if you haven't already. Use the guides in this book or build your own. It doesn't matter what they are as long as they make you feel good and can become part of your daily life.

My five wellness tools

These are the five wellness tools I use daily:

- *Exercise:* I do some form of exercise daily. Usually, I have six days of relatively intense sessions followed by a rest day that also involves a long walk.

- *Meditation:* 2 × 20-minute sessions per day using transcendental meditation (more on that below).

- *Perdekamp Emotional Method (PEM):* I recently learned an acting technique called PEM, which stands for Perdekamp Emotional Method. It was developed and designed by

German director and playwright Stephan Perdekamp and is a method based on a biological process. It's one of the best acting techniques I have come across, not only helping with performance, but also as a tool for daily life. Basically, you use science-based practices to access your emotions by learning how to breathe and moving your face and body in different ways. It's now been used successfully to help people in careers of all kinds and even with autistic children to help them access emotions. I have an amazing teacher and I really can't recommend this technique more highly.

- *Gratitude journalling:* I got into this in recent years after hearing many people talk about the benefits of practising gratitude. I simply write down three things in the notes in my phone that I'm grateful for each morning. I love doing this so much, I've made it part of your task at the end of this chapter.

- *Breathing:* I practise breathing exercises, which I also had to learn for acting. We often unlearn how to breathe properly, but we're actually meant to breathe from our belly. It feels weird at first, but it's amazing how much more oxygen you take in when you breathe properly. I practise this every morning and it really sets my mind for the day.

PATHWAY 4 | STILL YOUR MIND

Internal vs external

It's impossible to maintain a sense of wellbeing if you base your happiness on external events. Sure, it's great to achieve goals, and, as I've discussed, I'm not saying it's negative to aim for the stars, but what is dangerous is basing your self-worth on outside factors. There's an endless list of what those factors can be, and I've included a few examples (overleaf).

Do these ring any bells with you?

- If only I had more money.

- I want to be more famous.

- I won't be good enough until I get a job promotion.

- I thought I was successful until I met my more successful neighbour.

- I'm not attractive enough.

- Once I have a family, house and car, I can finally be happy.

The list can go on forever. And there are real-life examples all around us of people who are still unhappy despite achieving all the external things they said would make them happy. I've met extremely wealthy people, many who have opened up to me saying they're desperately unhappy and that all the money didn't make them any happier. Many celebrities have drug-related issues, and some have died from overdose or by suicide.

The simplest way around this is to work out what you value and care about. For example, if you're a chef and are ambitious, your value could be, 'I want to make the best quality food that I can, everyday'. That value is directly tied to you and doesn't require you to acquire anything from others. It may or may not lead you to become the most successful chef in the world, but regardless, you'll be content and happy from day one if you simply focus on making the best quality food each day.

We can all come up with values for our own lives. As I outlined, I set mine as 'I want to make global change in mental health'. I live by this daily, and whatever I'm working on I remind myself that it doesn't matter the outcome, I'm just going to try and do things in a way that can help. It may only help one person, but it can still make a difference. I get to live my value daily and while it may lead to big things, it may also lead to small things. It doesn't matter—it's my personal value and it keeps me grounded.

A mindset of purpose

A good example is Joe Biden, the 46th president of the United States. He is a brilliant example of persevering against all obstacles, and of showing that having purpose is the one thing that helped him get through. After becoming one of the youngest senators in US history in his early 30s, he lost his wife and daughter in a car crash, with his two sons only just surviving the incident. He carried on, remarried, ran for president twice, eventually becoming vice president, lost his eldest son to cancer, and became president at the age of 78 after running for a third time.

He lived by a mantra of picking himself up and moving forward no matter what obstacles were in his way. This is a big part of what mindfulness is about. You can get so caught up in your own emotions you forget why you wanted to do something in the first place, and then give up. Mindfulness is being able to look at your life from a bird's eye view and making wiser decisions, despite the emotions you're currently feeling.

Scientific benefits of sleep

There's nothing like sleep to still your mind—it's the best! You feel refreshed and ready to tackle the day when you're well rested, while your body has worked hard the night before restoring and processing the day's activities.

The experts say you should aim for between seven and nine hours of sleep each night. It's also worth noting that if you exercise regularly, you'll need more than the minimum recommended hours to give your body time to repair and rejuvenate.

PATHWAY 4 | STILL YOUR MIND

According to SCL Health, sleep can:

- *boost your immune system.* When you give your body the sleep it needs, your immune cells and proteins can more easily ward off whatever comes their way, such as colds or the flu.

- *help stop you gaining weight.* If you're getting enough sleep, two hormones work together to prevent you from putting on weight (though they won't help you lose weight). If you don't get enough sleep, your body will produce a hormone called ghrelin, which boosts your appetite. Your body will also produce less of the hormone leptin, which tells you you've had enough to eat.

- *make your heart stronger.* Your heart needs rest to function properly and avoid problems such as high blood pressure and heart attacks. Lack of sleep means more of the stress hormone cortisol may be released, triggering your heart to work harder.

- *improve your mood.* Good sleep means waking up and feeling rested, with enough energy to get through the day without feeling stressed, angry or in a bad mood.

- *create increased productivity.* A good night's sleep can help you concentrate thanks to higher cognitive function.

- *increase exercise performance.* Sleep affects all types of exercise performance, helping with reaction time, muscle recovery and hand–eye coordination.

- *improve your memory.* A good night's sleep will help your mind process and consolidate everything that happened during the day much more easily.

Sleep and mental health

More research is emerging showing the impact that sleep (or lack thereof) has on our mental health, which can potentially lead to depression, anxiety, diabetes, stroke, heart disease, disrupted sleep and more. For example, studies by Harvard Medical School using different methods and populations estimate that 65–95 per cent of adult patients with major depression, and about 90 per cent of children with the disorder, experience some kind of sleep problem.

According to London-based science and technology magazine *New Scientist*, scientists have found that a rare mutation of the ADRB1 gene allows people to sleep for as little as three to four hours per night with no consequence to their health. It's a gene that affects high-profile people including The Rock (Dwayne Johnson) and Richard Branson, who talk about how they only need three to four hours of sleep, and then use the 'extra time' to work as a badge of honour. But this is rare and it's dangerous to apply this to your own life to perform at the same level. Unless you have this rare gene, you're likely to need seven to nine hours of sleep each night to maintain mental health.

Getting enough sleep

As many know, getting seven to nine hours' sleep each night is not that easy. Life is demanding and, like diet and exercise, sleep is one of the simplest things to neglect, despite knowing it's so good for us.

For example, you might have an important meeting you're unprepared for. In a last-ditch attempt, you stay up all night and only sleep for a couple of hours. But when you're ready to present, you're exhausted and can barely string a sentence together.

Other factors that can cause sleep problems include:

- money, housing or work problems

- sleeping somewhere uncomfortable or where you are easily disturbed

- sleep disorders

- being a parent or carer

- medication, recreational drugs and alcohol

- shift or night work

- current or past trauma

- mental and physical health problems.

It's important to practise good sleep hygiene. Keep it free from distractions such as phones and television screens, and use your bedroom for sleep and sex, and those alone. Make sleep a priority, and don't brush it off in place of things you think are more important.

Like everything in life, it comes down to balance. If you plan in advance, it's easier to avoid last-minute situations such as prepping for an exam or meeting. Just try to do your best to get enough sleep.

INSIGHTS FROM DR CARMEL HARRINGTON

Dr Carmel Harrington (PHD, LLB, BSC, DIPED) is a lawyer and educator who has been working in the world of sleep for more than 20 years. Carmel was one of the first guests on the Move Your Mind *podcast, and it turned out to be one of our most popular episodes! She is a world-leading sleep expert, and I couldn't think of anyone I would rather have contributing to this section.*

If you look at the research, sleep affects every part of your life. From your physical health and mental health to cognition and relationships. If you want to be energised, excited about life, have good relationships with people and be the best version of yourself, then you must respect sleep. And professionally, from a research point of view, we know it all depends on sleeping well.

Shakespeare said, 'It's the chief nourisher in life's feast'. Even 500 years ago, the importance of sleep was recognised. Furthermore, Benjamin Franklin was quoted to have said, back in the day, 'Early to bed, early to rise, makes a man healthy, wealthy and wise'. There is certainly a lot of science behind sleep, but history also tells us that we have always known how important it is. Sleep wasn't even studied seriously until around the 1950s, so scientifically, we are still learning new things.

What we know is that a long-term lack of sleep will make you five times more likely to develop depression and other mental health disorders, twice as likely to develop dementia and three times as likely to develop cognitive decline. You're also more likely to develop chronic illness such as diabetes, obesity and cardiovascular disease.

In the short term, lack of sleep can lead to poor immunity, leaving you vulnerable to colds, flus and infections. Our immune functions mop up foreign cells, bacteria and viruses, and this decreases by as much as 50 per cent after poor sleep. The biggest effect in the short term is the impact on cognition and behaviour. Even one or two days of poor sleep can make you cranky, foggy headed and lead to poor decision making, which you have probably experienced from time to time.

Right now, there's a lot of unpredictability in the world, which affects sleep. For example, COVID-19 has fuelled more anxiety in people, and more people are seeking a quick fix to problems by taking sleeping pills. The thing about sleeping aids is that they knock out your pathways, and you're not actually working within your own system. I'm not saying never have drug-induced sleep, but you should only use them if you absolutely must. We don't want to need drugs to sleep. People are using uppers and amphetamines, and about 30 per cent of people will suffer from insomnia at some point. Essentially, two-thirds of us are just not getting enough sleep.

It's also worth mentioning that less than one per cent of the population needs fewer than seven to nine hours of sleep (as a result of an uncommon gene). There are quite a few famous examples of high-profile people needing less sleep—Margaret Thatcher is often quoted. But we know that people who don't get the right amount of sleep over a period of time are likely to develop dementia and cognitive decline, and Margaret Thatcher did have dementia for quite some time. We don't really know if she had the gene, and it's only been lately that we've been able to test it.

Instead, we need to use science to show people there are healthier ways. Treat sleep as naturally as you do things like exercise and sunshine. Your brain and body love to feel safe, so the more routine you have when going to sleep, the more comfortable you will be to sleep. This needs to be introduced to children too, helping them to feel comfortable at bedtime, which is very important.

Discipline around device usage is also important. I worked with a couple who were always on their devices, and now they lock them away at 8 pm until the next day. It's become completely routine and their kids are now used to doing it as well, not seeing it as punishment.

Sleep myths and misconceptions

- *Alcohol helps you sleep:* Alcohol is a sleep stealer. If you drink enough it will help get you to sleep but you'll be unable to maintain it and your sleep structure will be significantly altered.

- *Exercise is more important than sleep:* Many people cut back on sleep to fit in a daily exercise routine, thinking that they are taking the 'healthy' option. However, there are three pillars of wellbeing — nutrition, exercise and sleep — and all are equally important. Sleep needs to be of equal priority to the other two.

- *We need less sleep as we age:* We should maintain seven to nine hours of sleep per night well into our old age. After the age of 65, sleep needs may decrease by about an hour, but many older people still require seven to nine hours.

- *It's abnormal to wake up during the night:* It's completely normal to have wakeful periods during the sleep period, and most of us spend up to 5 per cent of total sleep time in wakefulness.

- *You can catch up on sleep on the weekend:* When you constantly deprive yourself of sufficient sleep on weekdays, sleeping longer on the weekends may make you feel better and more energised. But research shows that this does not restore the health benefits of the sleep you've missed, and the cognitive effects of poor sleep can still be detected days after you catch up. For optimal health and performance, sleeping the right amount every night is critical.

Move Your Mind with Carmel: Manage sleep better

How you sleep at night is often dependent on how you spent your day. To maximise sleep you need to prepare both your body and your mind.

To prepare your body:

- get up at the same time every day

- exercise for at least 20 minutes per day (a walk at lunchtime is good)

- don't have caffeine after midday

- refrain from drinking alcohol

- don't sleep during the day (a nap of 20 minutes is okay)

- eat only a small meal at night and in particular, don't eat a big meal within three hours of bedtime

- don't exercise within three hours of bedtime (this will stimulate your body).

To prepare your mind:

- Deal with the issues of the day. In the early evening, spend no more than 20 minutes writing down events of the day that are of concern along with potential solutions. Then close your notepad and put it away.

- Set an alarm one hour before bedtime. At that time:

  - turn off all technology

  - dim the lighting in the room

- take a warm/hot shower

- do some relaxation exercises.

• Ensure the bed and bedroom environment is conducive to sleep, meaning it:

  - is quiet

  - is cool

  - is dark

  - contains absolutely no technology.

My approach: creating my own mantra

When my mind is trying to talk me out of something or catastrophise, I draw on all my experiences and remind myself that I can't control what my mind thinks. But I can decide what I give power to, and the core mindfulness lesson is that I don't allow all those thoughts to control me. Repeating this mantra of ignoring the thoughts in my mind over and over helps me to override the computer program in my head telling me negative thoughts or stories that aren't true. It's now burned a message into my mind that I can overcome anything and I use it every single time I have to deal with a challenging situation, regardless of what's in front of me. I can't recommend doing this highly enough—I do it daily and it's one of the most powerful things I've found. It's my mantra for life.

These experiences have conditioned my mind to not only deal with challenges, but also to seek them out, setting myself up to be rejected time and time again. Taking the harder road and acting with fear and rejection isn't easy, but the long-term benefit is always worth it. As discussed, I truly believe there is no such thing as failure, only achieving the desired outcome or learning a lesson, and I live my life by this. The only real fear I have is not following my heart or looking back and doing nothing. You can avoid it by making it your mantra to follow your gut, be bold and put yourself out there.

Acting

Acting is proof that there's no such thing as failure because being an actor involves a lot of rejection. You get sent auditions (often the night before), have to learn pages of dialogue, walk into a room of strangers with little preparation, and then bare your soul and emotions. You then hear nothing (most of the time) unless you land the role. I've often had five to 10 auditions in any week, and have seen many actors implode, overcome by stress and anxiety.

My meditation and exercise tools are critical for me to deal with this, using the mantra of ignoring the thoughts my mind tells me and looking at each audition as a chance to either land a role or learn something. And reminding myself that the right role will come when it's meant to.

One of the most famous actors in the world, Mark Ruffalo, is a good example. He talks about having done around 800 auditions before getting his big break. 800! Many major actors have a similar message: 'Don't quit!' But one story I love about perseverance is from Hollywood action man Sylvester Stallone. Desperate to make it in New York as an actor, he tried everything, but was struggling to make ends meet. Things got so bad he sold his dog to a man he met in a local store. It was during a fight featuring Muhammad Ali that an idea sparked, and he spent the next two days writing the entire script for the film *Rocky*. As he shopped it around, the studios loved it and threw money at him on one condition: they didn't want him as the lead because he was unknown and had a funny voice. But Stallone held firm. He turned down every offer because he believed that he should star in the film. The offers dried up, until one studio came forward with a $35 000 deal featuring him as the star. With the cheque in his hand, he returned to the store to get his dog back. After showing up every day, he finally saw the man he'd sold it to. He offered him double what he'd sold it for, but was knocked back. He kept persevering until he eventually paid $15 000 for his dog. Of course, *Rocky* went on to win an Oscar and this iconic role cemented Stallone's position as a Hollywood superstar. He's a great example of persevering against all odds—despite the failures, he never gave up.

I always say to people that whatever your dream is, it's likely to be 10 times harder and take five times longer than you expect. Rather than see this as a negative, embrace it and remind yourself that every obstacle takes you one step closer to achieving your dream. There's no magic formula—just good old blood, sweat and tears. You can do anything if you commit and put your mind to it.

Transcendental meditation (TM)

I have been practising transcendental meditation (also known as Vedic meditation) for many years. I discovered it when suffering severe anxiety during my experience on *Dancing with the Stars*. Yes, I already had my mantra and had learned mindfulness techniques, but I needed something else to help manage the acute levels of anxiety I was experiencing. It was so confronting. I didn't know how I would get through it, but I was introduced to a meditation teacher, and then TM, one of the oldest meditation techniques.

TM is a form of silent mantra meditation created by Maharishi Mahesh Yogi in the mid 1950s. It became popularised in the 1960s and 1970s with celebrities, and by the early 2000s, the worldwide TM organisation had been taught to millions, with spin-offs including products and programs.

Basically, I sit down and perform two 20-minute sessions per day repeating a personal mantra. This is given to me and I have to repeat it over and over in my head as I practise. Like anything, it's not the be all end all, but I find that the structure and discipline to sit for two rounds of 20 minutes daily, plus the simplicity of focusing on one mantra, really works for me. While on *Dancing with the Stars*, I would remind myself that no matter what happened, I would get to have my two rounds of meditation. It became a real crutch for me and allowed me to have time out to calm my mind with a rigid structure around it.

The benefits are vast and there is an enormous amount of scientific research showing TM can increase lifespan, reduce stress and anxiety, improve sleep, lower blood pressure, increase productivity, lower the risk of heart attack, and improve brain function and memory.

This was so effective in helping me deal with the overwhelm of that reality show that I kept practising it and found my mind being calm more and more over time. I've always come back to it and having these tools and daily practices under my belt has helped me to embrace fear and confront every situation I find myself in today.

Africa and India

I've been lucky enough to explore both Africa and India and met many locals who had very little. Despite this, they always seemed so joyful and embracing, with a happy presence about them. A couple of years ago I decided to challenge myself again and buy a one-way ticket to India, staying in an apartment in coastal Mumbai for a more authentic experience than living in a hotel. The owner, Abraham, and I got along like a house on fire and spent every evening chatting for hours, after visiting the local dining spots and bars. He was about 70 years old, with so much wisdom and an incredible sense of humour. I loved learning from him and absorbing everything he said.

We have stayed in touch, and not long after meeting him I landed a small, English-speaking acting role in one of the biggest Indian films being made that year, starring with one of their most successful actors, the late Irrfan Khan. It was in Mumbai, so I instantly emailed Abraham and was lucky enough to spend another 10 days at his place, picking up where we left off, and spending each night talking for hours on end.

Following my experience with Abraham, I travelled all over the country and met more locals. The same thing struck me—the joy and happiness they showed despite having very little. Most of the people I met would be lucky to find enough food and water to get through the day and the only thing they worried about each day was looking after their loved ones and surviving.

They didn't have the option to think 'Why does my friend have a more expensive car?', 'I wish I had more money and a different job', 'I want to live in a new city', or 'I wish I was more famous and had more social media followers'. None of that existed to them, so they didn't have the luxury to indulge in those thoughts, which ultimately became a positive thing.

Having too much choice is a major Western problem and while we think it's a luxury and our right to have everything we want in life, the problem is that it creates a need to always want more, and to try and compete with others, which can lead to severe unhappiness.

The locals I met in Africa and India had naturally learned how to be present and truly value the important things in life: family and health. The example they set is that we can never have everything, so why worry about trying to have it all? Why not accept where you are right now, embrace it and make the most of it? Sounds logical, yet few of us live by this mindset. If we could somehow learn to do this,

PATHWAY 4
STILL YOUR MIND

we would make life simpler, become better people and ultimately lead happier lives.

Performance anxiety

I had major issues around sleep when I was competing as an athlete. I was anxious about ensuring I got enough sleep to perform at the level I needed to. But combined with the unhealthy levels of training from a very young age, not getting the right amount of sleep only added to the problem. I remember lying in bed terrified I wouldn't get the sleep required to perform the next day. The more I worried, the worse it became, and the less sleep I got.

The night before a competition I'd panic about potentially not getting enough sleep. I'd even go to bed two to three hours earlier than usual hoping it would allow me enough time to eventually get to sleep. It didn't work. I'd lie in bed and the only thing I could focus on was the fact that I was still awake. It led to compulsive thoughts and desperation at trying to fall asleep, sometimes resulting in only getting one hour of sleep and having to compete the next day.

I would kick myself after the competition, which would only cause me to further obsess about not getting to sleep. This went on and on and like other mental health–related issues, I learned that focusing on the problem almost never works. I needed to learn to accept what was happening when I would struggle to sleep and remind myself that no matter what, everything will be okay. Eventually this broke the cycle as it removed pressure, allowing me to sleep properly.

If I ever find myself tossing and turning, I now just accept it and allow whatever is happening to happen. If I have an important talk or meeting first thing in the morning and am struggling to sleep, I remind myself that it will be okay and that I can't control the situation. Whatever happens will happen, and I know from experience that in every single situation I have ever worried about, things have always turned out okay.

A final word

Like many situations in life, I've found the best way to learn and become more mindful is through experience and confronting situations head on. Whether I've fallen flat on my face or succeeded, I've learned a little more each time and used the experience to shape my life for the better.

As I keep repeating, it doesn't matter if things don't go your way, but what does matter is not trying and letting your mind control you. You can't control what you think about, but you can control how you respond. As I've said, there's no shame in failing, but what will eat away at you is not doing anything at all.

Using my five wellness tools, and my other mindfulness and sleep techniques, helps me with this every day.

Move Your Mind with Nick: Start practising mindfulness

- *Practise gratitude.* As I mentioned earlier, practising gratitude is one of my five wellness tools. Write down three things you are grateful for straight away in the morning, right before bed or any time of the day that suits you. Try to do it daily. You can list the same three things every day, or you can come up with new answers. It could be anything, such as, 'I'm grateful for my family', or 'I'm grateful for the fresh air I'm breathing' or even 'I'm grateful that the sun came up today'. The key is to embrace the thought and remind yourself of your good fortune. Set the alarm on your device or use another form of reminder to help you remember to complete the task each day.

(continued)

- *Observe your mind.* Be mindful throughout the day and see if you can find any harmful thought patterns you would like to change. You may notice that you always worry about the future, or perhaps you're a very harsh critic of yourself when you don't see immediate results. When you catch your mind thinking a limiting thought, consciously replace the negative idea with its positive counterpart. For example, 'It's all right to be a beginner. I am already enough. I can get better with practice and time. I believe in myself. The future will have its challenges, but I am pro-actively solving problems in the *now*'.

- *Take a cold shower.* I know it's not as extreme as an ice bath, but it's much easier to organise and the health benefits are enormous. They include:

  - increased circulation

  - increased endorphins

  - improved metabolism

  - helping to fight off illnesses.

- *Listen to a guided meditation.* You can find hundreds of these to follow on YouTube, and on apps such as Headspace.

- *Accept the fear.* The next time you find yourself in a difficult or uncomfortable situation, rather than running from it or letting it overwhelm you, look at it as an opportunity to grow. Accept the fear and remind yourself that every time you face that fear you will take major steps forward. You'll be surprised how much change can happen with this mindset!

- *Let go.* Challenge yourself to let go of something that's playing on your mind. Remind yourself that you can't control most situations and letting go doesn't mean failure—it allows you to move forward to new things.

- *Do something kind once a week.* Again, expect nothing in return and notice the positive benefits this brings.

PART IV
THE THREE STAGES OF SUSTAINABLE CHANGE

First, I want to thank you for staying with me so far. Remember, this book is your mental health bible, so keep coming back to it and let's make continued change together.

Second, you've come a long way. Well done! Over parts I to III, you covered a lot of ground exploring the many different aspects of mental health and wellbeing: from sleep to exercise, connections, stillness and food … and everything in between. You explored mental health holistically, read shared personal stories and insights from experts, and learned tasks, tips and tools to take action in your own life.

As a result, you have a great base to start making a real difference in your life. And a strong foundation upon which to build ongoing change to your wellbeing.

But let's not stop there. Let's aim even higher! Now you're ready to take everything you've learned and apply it in three stages. You can have the best information and intentions in the world, but without focus, discipline and daily work, you're unlikely to turn it into long-term progress.

Part IV will help you do just that. It will equip you with long-term systems and habits for applying the learnings from parts I to III. It's the daily work, the continuous improvement and sustained efforts over the long term that will help you move towards your mental health goals. This part will give you daily action plans and steps to maintain continual improvement for life—enabling you to live the very best version of yourself (which is the subject of chapter 9).

In chapters 10 to 12, we'll work through three key stages for sustaining change: 'Make a plan', 'Do the work' and 'Check in'. You'll also find worksheets, which you can either fill out directly in the book or download from nickbracks.com/moveyourmind. They're designed to be used now and into the future, whenever you need them and depending on what clicks the most with you.

I THINK FACING DEATH, YOU HAVE A CHOICE: YOU CAN EITHER ACCEPT IT AND GO, OR YOU CAN FIGHT. THE FIRST WAS CERTAINLY NOT AN OPTION FOR ME.

Vincent De Luca OAM

CHAPTER 9

SET YOURSELF UP AND LIVE YOUR BEST LIFE

In this chapter, I want to touch on two words that will help bring everything in part IV into sharp focus: meaning and purpose. While I've mentioned them a few times in the book, they're crucial for helping you establish longer term success.

Meaning and purpose

If you're constantly trying to achieve things purely for yourself and your ego, then the meaning is likely to be insignificant. However, if you're trying to change the lives of others, whether that be through helping a friend, raising a family, caring for a loved one, putting your best foot forward at work and setting an example, or looking after the local community, your meaning and purpose will be deep and rich.

I urge you to truly identify your meaning and purpose while exploring these final chapters. It will help you get clear on using actionable steps to put into practice. Furthermore, the meaning and purpose you have now may change over time, so keep checking in and asking yourself tough questions.

Often, meaning and purpose come from things bigger than ourselves. Here are some great questions to start the ball rolling:

- If money didn't exist, what would you dedicate your time to?

- What inspires you?

- What are you passionate about?

- What will you regret not doing when you look back on your life?

- What are your strengths and weaknesses?

- What are you willing to improve upon?

- What do you want people to remember you for?

- What mark do you want to leave on the world?

- What would make you proud of yourself?

- Would you still be willing to follow the same career if you didn't receive praise and adulation? Are you proud of yourself behind closed doors?

Key learnings

Taking daily action while following your passion and being true to yourself will get results.

1. If you want to sustain your efforts, you need to make continual improvements over time. You must set yourself up for success.

2. Everything in life involves conditioning. You need to learn to train your mind to make change for life. And one of the best ways to do this is to create actionable steps.

INSIGHTS FROM VINCENT DE LUCA

Vincent De Luca OAM is a social worker, counsellor and lawyer who has worked in youth welfare, suicide prevention, and drug and alcohol prevention since he was a teenager. He has overcome terminal cancer twice, and in the 2004 Queen's honours list was the youngest Australian to be awarded the medal of the Order of Australia. I met Vince a few years back through our mutual interest in mental health. We have since become close friends and he has been an incredible support. He is one of the most generous and giving people I have ever met.

It was 1999 and I was 21, and standing for my first ever election for government. I was rushing around campaigning and I had lost a lot of weight. I thought it was just the business of campaigning, but my doctor said I probably had a stomach ulcer. I didn't think anything of it until anything I ate, I'd throw up. I was doing an interview with a journalist who I didn't like, and I threw up on her, which was opportune, but I thought it was just nerves. I decided to go back to the medical centre that day, where I was told I had

(continued)

a 28 cm tumour on the right side of my chest: 'A soccer ball–sized tumour is wrapped around your heart and lungs. So, we suspect you have six weeks to live,' they told me. It was very emotional, a big shock and I didn't know what to do.

I was told I had advanced Hodgkin's cancer and they'd given me six weeks to live. I was admitted to hospital that night and was put on high doses of chemotherapy, along with radiotherapy. It was a traumatic time. It changes you, and you lose your identity because you lose your hair, you can't eat, you can't move, you're tired and you're bleeding.

Seeing the emotion from those close to me was actually more traumatic than me going through it, but keeping busy and having the support of so many people kept me going. I thought to myself, 'Stuff this, it's not gonna kill me', and I kept busy. There was a determination and outright refusal that I was not going to die. I had things to do. I kept working in suicide prevention, along with politics, and this helped keep me going. I did welfare work from the hospital bed, and we did a fundraiser and donated money for a new medical device.

The cancer came back a year later. Again, they gave me six weeks to live. They said I had no chance and that I should go into palliative care, and I had to go through chemotherapy and radiology all over again. I also had an autologous skin cell transplant, where they practically kill you with chemo to ensure that there's no cancer in the body.

At the time, I was still studying. I had graduated from my Bachelor of Arts, Politics and History and I was still studying Law. When it came back, no-one thought I would survive, but I simply refused to go. It took years to build back my confidence and re-find my identity, but because I had maintained relationships, kept working and helping with causes and had my family and friends supporting me, I was able to eventually bounce back.

I think facing death, you have a choice: you can either accept it and go, or you can fight. The first was certainly not an option for me. I wanted to continue; I was going to fight no matter what, even though the pain throughout it was excruciating, both mentally and physically ... you can't describe the level of pain. It is that invasive and it's horrible and to lose your whole identity and have your body go up and down has a huge impact on your confidence levels. People don't recognise you.

My experience has made me more determined to fight for better conditions for people such as patients and nurses, and certainly not to waste time. It also taught me who you can trust, how to be loving, to show love, and accept love back, and that sometimes you can't necessarily help everyone. I have a very close friend network and a very close family, and I don't have time for bullsh*t. If I see someone being completely unreasonable, disloyal or jealous, I just move on and don't worry about what people think. Fortunately, I have met some brilliant, wonderful people in my life and I'm lucky to have so many supporters.

You now have the knowledge and the tools to help you live your best life. Chapters 10 to 12 will help you put them into practice long term.

ALWAYS REMIND YOURSELF THAT YOU HAVE TIME AND YOU DON'T HAVE TO DO EVERYTHING AT ONCE.

CHAPTER 10

STAGE 1:

MAKE A PLAN

Without a plan, there's no starting point. This chapter is about setting your objectives and goals, and getting clear on your processes. Your plan doesn't have to be perfect and will usually evolve as you move forward, but you want to make the best decisions you can with what you have available and go from there.

By now, you've read through the ways I've adapted my plans based on life events. I wanted to be an elite athlete and built my psyche around that being the only option for me. I gave it everything and eventually had to quit due to debilitating injuries. Rather than accept this and adapt, I fought against it, became depressed and abused alcohol to escape. This was a very unproductive and illogical approach. Then, I had no idea what I wanted to do but was faced with the challenge of having to overcome my fear of public speaking. Again, I was fighting against having to confront this fear and I can still remember so clearly vomiting beforehand. I also launched three companies simultaneously while still pursuing other endeavours, which wasn't impossible, but limited resources could only get me so far.

Initially, all of these experiences came at incredible personal, health and mental cost and I fought it every step of the way. But little did I know that being open to these experiences was paving the path for my future. And the experiences where I was open to change took off and led to new changes and experiences.

If you stick to your original plan without building in any flexibility, it's much harder to succeed. Instead, be open to change. It doesn't mean you shouldn't have specific goals and plans, but equally be open to adapt your plans. You never know what's around the corner and it's impossible to have all the answers. Whenever you start a new pursuit, the hardest thing is always actually starting. So, stop overwhelming yourself and thinking about the end goal. Stop worrying about getting it right. Stop trying to find the perfect plan. Just take that very first step and the rest will follow.

Baby steps

By first step, I mean baby steps, and I want to reiterate the importance of this. Because no matter what you're trying to change, you need to keep it simple and start off with the basics.

What I've learned is that you can do everything, just not all at once. Life is long and made up of seasons. Breaking tasks into smaller, bite-sized chunks is critical. Always remind yourself that you have time and you don't have to do everything at once. When I realised this, I started to see better results and feel less overwhelmed. I looked at what was available to me and broke things down into levels of importance. I now only focus on one (or two at most) main goals at a time. The rest can wait until the goals in front of me solidify. Why try and move on to new tasks when you haven't even mastered the one in front of you?

Setting goals

Goal setting is critical for anything you've set your mind to. If you're not clear on your goals or they're ambiguous or you're trying to do too much at once, you're unlikely to be successful. Instead, work out what you want to achieve long-term, dream big and aim for the stars.

However big your list is, you need to start somewhere. So, put every single thing down that comes to mind. Whether it's one or 30—it doesn't matter, just put it all down. You also need to be realistic. What are your first steps? What is realistic for you to achieve based on where you're at right now? For example, there's no point trying to become an astronaut if your goal is to enter space within the first 12 months. You need to break down the steps, research what's required and be brutally honest with yourself about the reality of how long it's going to take to achieve it. I often ask people to write down everything that's important to them right now that they want to change. Here are some examples:

- I want to exercise more

- I want to start my own business

- I want to lose 10 kilograms

- I want to travel for a year

- I want a promotion at work

- I want to spend more time with my family

- I want to save more money

- I want to help more people.

Once you've written down all your points, highlight the single most important thing you want to change right now. Just one single thing.

Put the rest of the points to the side and don't move on to mastering a new task until the one at hand gets the attention it deserves. Doing this will lead to focus, a higher chance of results and an increase in confidence once you move on to new tasks. I can't stress how effective and beneficial this can be.

Finally, anything worth doing takes time, refined skills and careful planning. Time frames are important when it comes to setting goals, so you need to have an end date and give yourself a cut-off point for when to move on if you're unable to make your goal a reality. Whenever you're setting out on a personal endeavour, such as starting a business, remember that you should allow for it to be 10 times harder and take five times longer than you expect. Of course, this may not be the case, but regardless, expect a challenge and prepare to face everything that gets thrown at you! And whether it's daily, monthly, yearly or five-yearly, if you persevere, stick to your plan and set goals, the results will come.

We met Dr Richard Chambers in chapter 2. He is a clinical psychologist and mindfulness expert, so I asked him to contribute his thoughts to the final chapters of the book. Here's what he has to say about making a plan.

Key points from Dr Richard Chambers

- You need a plan, no matter how motivated you are. Without one, you'll quickly get off track.

- Planning, like anything, takes practice.

- Set aside the time to plan and try not to be complacent.

> - Always check in on your progress. If things are going well, you might feel that you can take your foot off the brake, but this is often when you fall back off track.
>
> - Keep yourself accountable. If you have mentors and people keeping you accountable, you'll be much more likely to stick to your plans.
>
> - Make it fun! We can get so caught up in putting pressure on ourselves that we forget to enjoy the process. Remind yourself that there is a solution to every problem.

How to set goals

I use a handy tool to set my goals; it's an acronym: SMART. It's easy to remember and it's a simple reminder when setting your goals. The letters stand for:

- *Specific goals:* This is about being very specific. Remember, this can change over time, but at the beginning the more specific your goals are the better.

- *Measurable goals:* This is about creating time frames and exact dates/milestones around your goal. Without being specific you can lose focus and are less likely to achieve your goals.

- *Attainable goals:* It's important to set goals you can achieve. If you're trying to chase a goal that is virtually impossible, it will erode your confidence and you'll likely quit and give up on chasing other goals. On the other hand, don't make it too easy. If it's easy, it's not likely to extend you to reach your full potential. Find goals that are a major challenge but achievable.

- *Relevant goals:* Goals should be relevant to what you want to achieve and where your interest/skillset lies. There's no point trying to achieve something that's of no interest to you or isn't in line with what you want out of life. Stay focused on what you really want.

- *Time-based goals:* If you don't set a time frame on a goal it can drag on for years and you'll lose the urgency to put in the work. Keep up a sense of urgency and work hard. If things don't work out, there's still a chance to learn and find a new, even more relevant goal.

Move Your Mind with Nick:
Make a plan

Remember that putting your goals in writing will make them more attainable, and you more accountable. Also remember that having a plan will remind you of why you started in the first place and to keep pushing forward despite what gets thrown at you. It will never be an easy process, but if you keep putting in the work it will eventually happen. And, it goes without saying, set goals that inspire, excite and motivate you. Ensure they're something you're willing to fight for no matter what's thrown your way. To help you set your goals, I've created four worksheets. Each one is for making one simple change at a time, and then daily, weekly and monthly goal setting. They're great to refer to so you can keep on track with your progress.

CREATING HABITS ONE SIMPLE CHANGE AT A TIME

Start by reviewing what you want to change and selecting the most important. The goal is to do a small amount towards the change each day, and to stick to the pattern for a minimum of 21 days.

For example:

What is one thing you want to do more of?

Examples:
· Do 20 push-ups
· Cook with my family
· Say 'Hello' to the neighbours

What is one thing you want to do less of?

Examples:
· Putting yourself down
· Less screen time / social media
· Stop gossiping about others

What lifestyle change would you like to make?

Decided on your goal? Now use the 21-Day Habit Tracker (see page 223) to mark your progress and to spot patterns, like regular missed practices. Once your new habit is created, pick the next lifestyle change you want to make, and repeat this process to achieve it.

DAILY PLANNER

Track your sleep, exercise, meals, goals, and other regular patterns, and record your reflections with this daily planner. Use the 21-Day Habit Tracker (see p. 223) to help get used to filling this in each day.

Nick's Tip:
Set regular reminders on your phone to prompt you to fill in your planner as you go, instead of doing it all at the end of the day.

My goal for today:	Exercise for the day:	How many hours' sleep did I get last night?

What I am looking forward to today?	Meals for today?

Schedule	To-do list
	☐
	☐
	☐
	☐
	☐
Note	What did I learn today?
What am I grateful for?	My goals for tomorrow:

MY GOALS FOR THE WEEK

Use this planner to set smaller, short-term goals, develop your strategy for behaviour change, and monitor your progress and commitment. You can use the 21-Day Habit Tracker to record your progress, and turn short-term behavioural changes into long-term habits.

Week of:

Work goals

Personal goals

Happiness goals

Wellness goals

What steps I am taking to achieve my goals

What were the challenges? What did I learn?

MY GOALS FOR THE MONTH

Use this planner to set more ambitious goals, develop your strategy for behaviour change and monitor your progress. This planner works best when combined with the 21-Day Habit Tracker (see p.223).

Nick's Tip:
For long-term goals, keep a folder with blank copies of this planner and the 21-Day Habit Tracker. After 21-days/month, date and sign your completed worksheet, store it, and start a new sheet. Repeat as needed to reach your big goal.

Month of:

Work goals

Personal goals

Happiness goals

Wellness goals

What steps I am taking to achieve my goals

What were the challenges? What did I learn?

NO MATTER WHAT YOU'RE TRYING TO CHANGE IN YOUR LIFE, IF YOU CAN'T CREATE SUSTAINABLE HABITS, YOU'LL BE LESS LIKELY TO STICK TO YOUR GOALS AND MAKE LONG-TERM CHANGE.

CHAPTER 11

STAGE 2:

DO THE WORK

Now that you've set your goals and made a plan, it's time to get to work. This is the focus of stage 2: 'Do the work'. This is where you action your plans.

There are a few ways you can put your plans, goals and objectives in action before making them sustainable. There are three areas I'll focus on: PERMA™, creating healthy habits for life and resilience.

As you go about establishing a new pattern of behaviour, the part of your brain that wants to detect potential threats and ways to conserve energy will be activated. Don't be surprised if you experience fear and discomfort as you journey into the unknown, and don't give in to the negative emotion. You're safe — you can do this!

Remember to reward yourself for every small victory on the path to your goal. Be the encouraging parent who cheers on their toddler with every shaky step. Reward yourself in a more significant way when you finally achieve your goal, and you'll strengthen the new habit by helping your brain to associate habit building with joy and satisfaction. Brains like to repeat behaviour associated with pleasure and satisfaction!

It takes daily persistence to make or break a habit. But regular practice doesn't have to drain you. As little as five minutes is enough to allow a new pattern to set in your brain and body. Be warned: if you push yourself too hard, too soon, you're more likely to become overwhelmed and fall off the bandwagon. It's great to have good intentions, all the right equipment and amazing teachers, but habit formation requires patience and restraint, as well as commitment and support. Get together with a friend and be each other's cheerleader. Hold each other accountable by keeping records together. Meet up and discuss your goals, mistakes and lessons learned along the way.

PERMA™

Like the SMART tool, PERMA is another acronym. I've been using the PERMA model for about ten years and it's been incredibly helpful. In fact, much of my work over the past decade has stemmed from my initial learnings while delivering the PERMA model into organisations. It continues to be fundamental to my work today.

The concept was developed by Martin Seligman, one of the leading psychologists in the world. He is an American educator and author, and is well respected among scientific and clinical psychologists for his work in positive psychology.

When you're trying to learn something new and make big changes, it can be completely overwhelming. But the PERMA model drills down to five elements of wellbeing that can dramatically improve your life if you practise them regularly. It simplifies your wellbeing really well and is an everyday reminder of what you can do to create small daily changes. I've used it over the years to establish daily habits that are now second nature to me, regularly referring back to it to check in with myself and ensure I'm staying on track. It is embedded into both my life and work, and you'll see a natural thread of the PERMA principles throughout the learnings in this book.

PERMA is an acronym for five key principles—positivity, engagement, relationships, meaning and achievement.

Positivity

Our brains are wired to look for the negatives. Instead, we need to look for the positives. It sounds simple, but to improve the quality of our lives, we need to listen carefully to our thoughts before reacting to situations. If you can change something to a positive on a daily basis, you'll dramatically improve your quality of life and your performance too.

Here's an example. Have you ever gone to bed at night and your mind has run wild thinking about all the negative things that are happening or could happen in your life? And how many times have these thoughts actually become reality? More often than not, they remain just that, thoughts. And the more experience you have in dealing with the negative and overwhelming thoughts, the more you can learn to dismiss them and understand there's limited truth behind them. That's what positive emotion is about.

It means that when those negative emotions and thoughts pop up, you'll have the foresight to see that the negatives have no positive benefit, and that reframing them into a positive can make the world of difference. Most of the time, negative thoughts just get in the way of putting your best foot forward.

Engagement

This one's about being present and focused on whatever it is that you're doing at that moment. It doesn't mean dismissing something that's occupying your mind, but rather putting it to one side to concentrate on one task at a time. It could be something as simple as listening properly to a conversation or being at work and not feeling consumed by the list of tasks you need to tick off. Just focus on one thing and you'll be surprised at how gratifying it feels, plus you're more likely to get the job done in half the time.

This really boils down to the principles of mindfulness and meditation, which are the subject matter of chapter 8. It's about training your brain, which in this day and age is challenging given that concentration spans are at an all-time low. A study by Microsoft showed that in the year 2000, the average human attention span was 12 seconds. Look forward two decades and the average human attention span went down to around eight seconds. That's a decrease of four seconds in approximately 20 years. Where are we heading? The average attention span of a goldfish is said to be seven seconds!

For example, if I'm writing an important email for work, chances are I'm going to be distracted and lose focus if I'm checking my phone, looking at social media, messaging friends, worrying about what I'm cooking for dinner that night and looking at other websites. Instead, if I turn off all distractions and allow myself to fully focus only on that task, I will likely complete it in half the time and it will be twice as good.

I'm not saying you should ignore the other issues, but it's more about trusting that you will address those issues when the time comes. Research also shows that when you are fully focused on one task at a time, even if it's a task you hate, you're going to enjoy it more and feel more satisfied. It feels good to focus!

Relationships

Are your relationships healthy or not? It's a good opportunity to take stock of who you think plays an important role in your life—whether friend, family or work colleague. Unfortunately, some people are toxic. They constantly put you down and make you feel bad about yourself, and perhaps it's a relationship that you don't want to admit is harmful for you. On the other hand, if we're around positive, uplifting people, we will feel good about ourselves, energised, and aim for bigger and better things in life.

It may sound trivial, but relationships play one of the biggest roles in deciding whether we become successful, and have quality personal lives and peace of mind. Remember, never do nothing. You need to be able to recognise what's happening to you and to have the tools to walk away from it or try to confront it and improve the relationship.

It's a natural part of life for friendships to change and to grow apart from people. Relationships and people evolve and either grow together or drift apart. Both are fine. It's up to you to allow this process and not to feel guilty for doing what's best for you. The same rule applies to work too, and whether relationships are affecting you in a negative way. If they are, then look at how you could approach fixing them. If you feel you're being unfairly treated but don't know what to do about it, then talk to someone you trust and get advice. Surround yourself with people who are going to add value to your life.

A good way to look at a friend or partner is:

- Do I feel better after spending time with this particular friend?

- Am I reliant on my partner to make me happy and feel good?

- Can I cope without them?

- Do I feel constant fear of them leaving me?

Meaning

What's important in life? We get so caught up looking at what's up next, or the quick fix, that we forget about what it is we really enjoy doing. It's good to take a step back and remember that things take time.

The saying that all good things come to those who wait is true. Also, work isn't everything. I talk a lot about how external things can't be the answer and that we need to find peace from within, but there's also plenty of great stuff outside work that can help you get out of that fixed mindset. Doing something outside of yourself and setting aside time to do it is very powerful. We can all find things that are meaningful and important in life.

Meaning doesn't have to be directly derived from the activity or job at hand. You may not love your job, but find meaning in it because it allows you to support your family or follow a passion. You may hate exercise, but find meaning in the longevity it brings to your health and the weight loss that comes from it. It's important to spend time regularly looking for what you find meaningful in life and remind yourself what you care about. Gratitude journalling is an amazing way to do this and you can use the tools provided in chapter 12 to help you. Keep reminding yourself what your bigger meaning is when times are tough. You're always going to have rough days, weeks, months or years, but you can build resilience by referring to the PERMA model and learnings throughout the book. And if you can't find meaning, create it. Try a new skill. Do some social work. Help a charity. Anything that brings you outside of yourself and helps others is likely to bring some meaning!

Achievement

This one's about taking a step back and acknowledging what you've had to go through to achieve something. You don't need to throw a party or make a grand gesture, just pause to think about the steps you went through to get to your goal, what you had to overcome and the hardships you went through. Giving yourself a big pat on the back will increase your confidence and make you more likely to aim higher next time, because you've proven to yourself that you've done it before. This goes for both big and small achievements. Whatever it is, you should give yourself credit for what you had to overcome to achieve certain things. And never compare yourself to others. Everyone is on a different journey and what you achieve is personal to you, your own goals and what you had to overcome to get there.

Key points from Dr Richard Chambers

- The absence of mental illness is not just the definition of mental health. It's so much more than that, which can be enhanced in a simple and practical way by practising the PERMA principles every day.

- Doing this every day will slowly start to retrain the brain, moving away from the negative thoughts that we are naturally predisposed to, towards a happier, more efficient life that orients us to better opportunities — to our values and connections.

- The brain constantly changes, and you can retrain your brain to operate in more helpful ways. The moment you begin to activate a new part of the brain by doing an activity, it starts to get stronger. If you repeat activation over time (by practising a behaviour), those activated neural circuits become reliable and efficient — and a habit forms.

- Doing a little bit each day is what makes the difference. Remember that any progress, no matter how small, is valuable and can be built into massive change over time.

- Human beings are creatures of habit. 'We are what we repeatedly do', as Greek philosopher Aristotle said.

Creating healthy habits

Do you want to change your lifestyle significantly? To start a new routine without falling back into the same old pattern of behaviour that's stopped you from reaching your goals in the past?

The art of creating a new habit is one of the most useful skills you can master. No matter what you're trying to change in your life, if you can't create sustainable habits, you'll be less likely to stick to your goals and make long-term change. We're hardwired to avoid change, but this survival mechanism no longer serves us in most situations.

In modern times, you're rarely in life-threatening situations and most things in life aren't as big of a deal as we make them out to be. While there are certainly stressful situations, most of the time we worry about things that aren't as significant as our minds make them out to be.

Having said that, the biggest barrier to making change and breaking habits is our mind. While there is debate around the exact scientific formula for making and breaking habits, it's broadly agreed that it takes around 21 days. By this I mean that it's not just 21 days of doing the new task here and there, but making a full commitment (daily if need be).

The same goes for breaking a habit. If you're trying to stop drinking alcohol, and not just drinking less for a period of time, a good timeline to work to is a month. Any habit I have created or broken I have stuck to for a month. If you think too far forward or put too much pressure on yourself, you're likely to get overwhelmed and stop before you begin.

A good trick to play on the brain is to make a deal with yourself. 'I will commit fully to this for one month and stop if I see no benefit after that.' Keep it simple. Every single time I have done this I have seen so much benefit that I have stuck to it long term. But it's also hard because it involves moving out of your comfort zone, applying extreme discipline and doing things you may not enjoy.

We live in a world of instant gratification where our minds are conditioned to seek instant results. Anything instant is never sustainable and you need to remind yourself that life is long and anything meaningful needs to be nurtured over time. After all, if everything was easy, then where is the meaning when you achieve it? The struggle is part of the process.

As I talk about embracing failure and changing the language from failing and winning to learning or getting the desired result, the same goes for creating habits and struggle. If you can reframe your thinking from looking at change as a chore and a complete struggle, to looking at it as a challenge taking you closer to your long-term goal, it will make the world of difference. It ties into the saying, 'No pain, no gain'. The main key to success is hard work, perseverance and never giving up: 'Don't quit' as I wrote in chapter 8. There are no shortcuts to meaning, purpose and doing things properly. So, learn to create habits and make long-term change in your life!

Resilience

Routine is vital when dealing with adversity. We're always going to face adversity in life in different ways — some more than others. But as I have spoken about in my personal story throughout this book, I wouldn't have coped with the difficult times in my life had I not had my daily habits of exercise, meditation and speaking to those close to me. These helped me build resilience over the years and taught me that I can overcome anything. It's a very empowering feeling.

Building resilience will also help you when it comes to comparing your life to others. Comparison really is the thief of joy. It's hard to feel content when you're constantly looking at your neighbour's bigger house. It's the same with opportunity and choice. It's a luxury to have an abundance of options, but this can often lead to feeling overwhelmed and suffering paralysis by analysis. As always, it comes down to your internal world and resilience, by making your own choices and decisions about how you decide what you want and what you need in your life. If you're constantly looking at what other people are doing or have, no matter how good your life is, you won't enjoy it. Although there is no one size fits all, and it's human nature to be curious and want to grow, you need to know when it's healthy and when it's affecting your mental health. Social media is one of the worst ways to fuel this. But by monitoring your usage, what you look at and expose yourself to, you can avoid a lot of negative and useless emotions.

Five keys to resilience

The following five tips are key to staying resilient, keeping a positive frame of mind when you feel overwhelmed and preventing burnout:

1. maintaining good relationships with family, friends and others

2. accepting circumstances that can't be changed

3. developing realistic goals and moving towards them

4. taking decisive actions in adverse situations

5. taking care of your mind and body with regular exercise while paying attention to your needs.

INSIGHTS FROM SUSIE ABROMEIT

Susie Abromeit is an American actor, singer and former profes-
sional tennis player, mostly known for her breakout role in
the hit Netflix/Marvel show **Jessica Jones,** *starring alongside*
Carrie-Anne Moss. Susie was ranked #6 in the U.S. in tennis
and in a full circle moment will next be seen alongside Will
Smith in **King Richard,** *a film based on the Williams sisters.*
I met Susie when I interviewed her on the **Move Your Mind**
podcast and felt compelled to share her story.

Looking back, problems arise when you have a predisposition
to mental health issues, and when you don't have the correct
environment. As a kid I had a lot of energy - I was the rambunctious
kid who would get into trouble. I would get sent to the principal's
office because I was always talking or not listening. I was a bit
of a class clown/troublemaker. In hindsight, I was reacting to a
lack of attention at home and so I was trying to get it at school
but, unfortunately, I was getting the wrong kind of attention. You
experience hierarchies in school (and life) as you move up and
down ladders. In Jordan Peterson's book he talks about lobsters
and the class of hierarchies and serotonin. The lobster who loses
in a fight is basically in a state of depression. This was relevant
to my life too.

And so I was stuck in this troublemaker pattern for many years.
I'm sure it wasn't easy on my parents as they both worked full
time from when I was two. It felt like I was constantly shuffled
from one thing to another or had a nanny at the time. When
all the kids would be picked up by their parents, I was left at
school and put into extended day care for several hours until
my mom could pick me up. Although there was a part of me that
accepted that this is the way it is, I could see other kids not only
didn't have the same problems I had, like getting in trouble, but
they were also picked up by their parents from school and not

(continued)

put in extra programs. When I would look around at the other kids in the after hours programs, it seemed we all had similar issues. I would see my parents for maybe an hour or two a day at most which had a slightly chaotic feeling — go to school, go here, do this, eat, sleep — and my parents always felt rushed as if there wasn't enough time in the day.

This kind of life probably wasn't the best for me. I was subconsciously getting the message of, 'Oh I'm not enough'. My parents were only just doing their best at the time, trying to pay the bills, live their own lives, but I think since I was so sensitive it really affected me.

It didn't help that I didn't fit in neatly with what the idea of a girl was. I was the talented artistic, tomboy, athlete who was also obsessed with boys. It seemed none of those things were helpful for me at the time. Although I was certainly encouraged by my mom and sister for my artistic and athletic ability, there didn't seem to be a place in school for me where I could really shine. It wasn't until my mother put me in tennis classes that I found a healthy outlet to put all of my extra energy into. And next thing you know, it was all I did. I would play tennis until my hands bled, because suddenly I was getting the attention I wanted. I had coaches surrounding my courts telling me I was going to be top ranked in New England. Long gone was the girl who was a troublemaker, who was put in extended day care with a bunch of other misfits. I felt like I was superhero. And somehow, now in fifth grade, I began to have more confidence, got straight A's, and was now popular as other kids saw this positive change too. In addition to that, I started dating Mr Popular. And then! Bam! I broke up with him.

And then I moved up to an age class in tennis, where I was now at the bottom. And as tribal as 6th grade can be, all my friends unfriended me to side with Mr Popular. I was getting bullied constantly by my former 'boyfriend' and his friends. Just about every single day they would say or do something brutal to me. Like when they tried to glue dog sh*t in my mailbox and tee-pee my house. I think about it now and laugh, but I can still feel the pain I felt then. And so I started to act out because of it. In sixth grade my mom had sent me to a psychologist and they were like, 'Oh you have ADHD'. They placed this label on me without properly looking at my life. It is a point I really want to hammer home: labels are harmful and we need to understand why people behave in the way they do.

I was grateful to have tennis to escape into at this point in my life. Despite all the challenges I was facing, it regulated my body and gave my mind something to focus on. I was finally able to channel that energy into something positive, eventually becoming the #6 ranked player in the US. I was sponsored by Nike, had a full tennis scholarship to my dream school Duke University, a top tennis school. But then, shortly after college, I entered into nine-year relationship that was really, really unhealthy. I didn't realise it at the time, but it was a #MeToo situation that you now read about. I don't want to go into too much detail—but basically it was sort of like a father-figure turned relationship-partner situation that was really unhealthy.

I can see how I fell into that toxic relationship. It started off much like a cult, A one man cult. It satisfied my childhood need and gave me all the attention in the world. They tell you how amazing you are, act as your biggest supporters, spend lots of money on you, and gain your trust after working with you for years. And then, slowly-but-surely, little-by-little, they tell you that your family and friends don't understand you. They use your insecurities against you, isolating you from the outside world and saying, 'Don't trust them. I'm the only one who understands you, knows you and knows what you need." And then, because you think they have your best interests at heart that childhood wound feels filled with what looks like love. They take more control, and next thing you know, you've dumped your current college boyfriend, gotten rid of all your friends, and you don't speak to your family anymore. And now, the only person you listen to is this one-man cult leader, who has full and total control of your life. And the whole time, it was as if they had this master plan of grooming you.

(continued)

By the time I had realized it was a problem, it was nine years too late. I was only 22 when I fell into that destructive relationship. It really felt like Stockholm syndrome. Like I was being gaslighted. I just didn't know any better. I thought I knew my worth, but when I came out of it, I didn't anymore. I realised 'Oh my God! I don't know what my world is!'. I had PTSD. It turned my world upside down, because the world I once knew was no longer. I had no idea what anything was anymore. Everything was now up for grabs. I found myself constantly obsessing over situations and it almost felt like I was stuck in an infinite nightmarish loop. You feel so tortured you fall into a dark hole or want to jump out of the nearest building. I was at my wits end and I definitely had moments of real darkness. I had two moments where I wanted to end it all because I couldn't get out of this terrible Black Mirror-like episode.

In my recovery, I tried everything from talk therapy, EMDR, going to Tony Robbins, going to Demartini classes, working with coaches, and going to Hoffman Institute. But it was Neurofeedback that allowed me undo a lot of the negative thought patterns that resulted from this. It heals concussions, anxiety, depression, ADHD, memory and migraines, and sleep. All the cousins of PTSD. Neurofeedback changed my life. Nothing else was as effective. I can't recommend it enough. It helps you practice mindfulness and move out of ruminating on thoughts. It allows you to finally let go.

My simple message to anyone struggling is this: There is hope on the other side. When I lost my house in the LA fires and was recovering I had a period where I just cried for hours each day for several months. Realizing that maybe God had put me in a time out, I finally felt safe enough to cry and cry for all the pain I went through in my life. Crying about all the trauma I had ever experienced. No longer trying to repress those feelings, and pretend I was fine. I was taught not to cry, but I was finally giving myself the space and time to process everything I had not allowed myself to feel. I have come to realize that it's so important to process trauma, and cry about it and re-experience it. To allow it to move through your body and be expelled, instead of disassociating from it and pretending those terrible things didn't happen to you. This energy had been stuck in my body for so so long. And once I allowed myself to truly feel it and experience it, I was then able to understand how and why those traumatic things happened, which meant I had a new understanding and awareness. I was now able to find the lessons in the trauma, which meant I could make different choices. But if I didn't process it, experience it, and then expel it, I would continue to repeat that trauma and never understand why I was stuck in those patterns.

This is essential if you want to overcome PTSD in a sustainable way. I wouldn't change anything as everything has led me to becoming who I am and has forced me to grow and evolve in ways I otherwise would not have. The recovery process is kind of like a rite of passage you have to go through. If you survive it, if you find the healing, then you can find a superpower. Finally, I would say that by just turning off the television. Limiting what news I view. Taking a step back and de-stimulating. I can now finally sit still and be with myself.

Move Your Mind with Nick:
Do the work

On the following pages you'll find worksheets to help you use PERMA as well as creating habits for 21 days. Use the habit worksheet to plan and record your experience as you work towards your goals. Make sure your habit-building experience is fun and exciting. Alternatively, choose a habit that is less important to you, but both fun and easy to pursue. If you are unused to creating habits, then the more relaxed you make the process, the more likely you are to stick to it. Remember, everybody has an off day (or week or month!) but it's never too late to get back on track and start the 21-day process again. Don't be too hard on yourself!

THE PERMA™ PRINCIPLES

Introducing the PERMA™ model, created by psychologist Martin Seligman. The PERMA model can be used together with the goal planners and the 21-Day Habit Tracker, to experience the benefits of increased wellbeing every day.

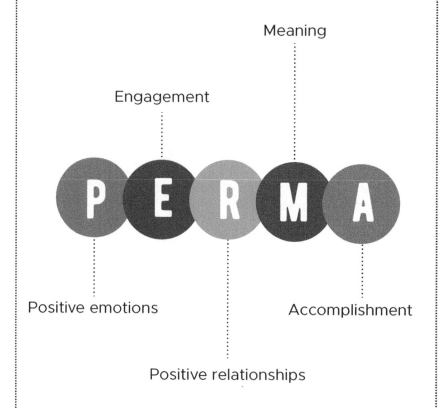

Meaning

Engagement

Positive emotions

Accomplishment

Positive relationships

Nick's Tip:
Refer to chapter 11 for a more in-depth explanation of the PERMA principles. When implementing PERMA principles in your life, remember that any progress, no matter how small, is valuable and can turn into massive change over time.

21-DAY HABIT TRACKER

Track your progress as you turn a goal into a habit. Colour in, tick off, or place a fun sticker in each box to mark your progress.

If you practice for 21 days in a row, your brain will begin to re-wire itself to include the new pattern in your day-to-day life. After 21 days, you can start another cycle to really strengthen that new behaviour.

If you miss practice, write down why. A small change might be all it takes to help you stay on track.

No time to practice on Wednesdays?
Split practise into 2 × 10 min sessions

Too tired after working overtime?
Practise before going to work

Kids interrupt when they see you focussing on something else?
Set up a fun activity for the kids or make a deal with your partner to watch kids while you practise.

> **Nick's Tip:**
> Make a note of your challenges. It will increase your self-awareness and help you 'hack' your schedule for performance, to save you time and stress, and to build your self-confidence.

1	2	3
4	5	6
7	8	9
10	11	12
13	14	15
16	17	18
19	20	21

Your notes about this experience:

WE ARE OFTEN LEFT DISSATISFIED BECAUSE WE SET OUR EXPECTATIONS SO HIGH THAT THEY BECOME UNATTAINABLE.

CHAPTER 12

STAGE 3:

CHECK IN

Making a sustained change to your mental health means a lot of things: dealing with major issues as they arise, raising self-awareness, helping others, and improving your performance and quality of life on a daily basis. While it's a lot to take in, these standards of living are achievable.

In stage 3, we explore how you can build repeatable behaviour change, and tools to help you take action. This stage is broken down into three areas designed to help you monitor your mental health over time—observation, facing fears and building happiness—each with worksheets to fill out or print off when you need them. This is about circling back and fine-tuning everything you've learned and set out to achieve for the future.

More important than learning the changes is practising and applying the tools over the long term. By constantly checking in, reviewing and repeating your foundation principles, you'll be able to keep going and give yourself powerful ownership of your mental health. As you know, repetition over time builds strong, healthy habits. So don't let all your good work go to waste!

Key points from Dr Richard Chambers

- There are so many things you can do to take care of yourself and have a better and more fulfilling life. All the techniques and tools in this book are designed to help you be happier, more successful, and to value and stay focused on what's important in life.

- Everyone has a unique story, and you can learn from the stories of the people around you. Take the principles others have applied to overcome their challenges and use them in your own life.

- Review the learnings and continue the process. Apply these new ideas to your life as you see fit. Enjoy finding your process!

Observation

Making weekly and monthly observations is a great way to check in with yourself, track your progress and tweak your goals. After all, things always change in life, obstacles come up, and your mindset will grow and change. By observing what happened at the end of the week or month, you can seek clarity on how to keep putting your best foot forward.

A great process is to revisit the activities you attempted from this book, and ask yourself:

- What did you find beneficial?

- What was difficult?

- What seems impossible?

- What have you learned from the book?

Make a note of what you responded well to, what you found challenging and what you're still trying to overcome. In time, you'll be able to see yourself complete goals that once felt impossible.

Facing fears

Facing fear is an essential part of life if you want to continually grow and prosper. When you're faced with difficult challenges that require you to act outside your comfort zone, you usually have two options: face the challenge (fight) or hide away (flight). It's innate to feel scared of failure and rejection, and it's a built-in survival mechanism that helped humans survive threats in the past. But nowadays, there are few things that really threaten your life, and the fears and potential rejections you often face on a daily basis are not putting your life at risk but rather represent opportunities to grow and move closer to your goals.

I often talk about how you need to view fear and failure in a different way. If you look at them in a black-and-white context—that you're failing if you don't get the result—you'll build incredible anxiety and not want to embrace the task. However, if you look at fear and failure as either giving you the desired result or helping you learn something—which are both positive outcomes—there's no downside. This simple change in thinking makes a world of difference. Believe me, I have tried it many times and reframing the thinking will change your life.

Here are some examples of how you can reframe your thinking:

- *Asking someone out*: They might say yes or they might say no. You can either look at the potential rejection as a sign you're not good enough, or frame it that if they say no, they're doing you a favour. You can now move one step closer to someone more suitable for you.

- *Applying for a new job*: If you get the job, then great, but if not, you can remind yourself that it's taking you closer to finding an even better one. No one thing is perfect.

- *Starting a business*: Many new businesses fail. You can either look at this as a negative or find the positive. The lessons learned from the unsuccessful business are key to finding an even more suitable one to focus on and apply the learnings to, and increasing your chance of success.

Building happiness

I've decided to end the book by talking about happiness, because at the end of the day, that's what it's all about, right? After many years, I've finally found my own inner peace where most of my days are full of meaning, purpose and joy. But, it's still a never-ending journey with constant ups and downs, and I have to work on this every single day.

The term 'happiness' is often seen as a destination tied to future events: 'I will be happy when I finally have a bigger house', 'I will be happy when I get married', 'I will be happy when I have my dream job', 'I will be happy when people applaud and admire me'... the list goes on. We are often left dissatisfied because we set our expectations so high that they become unattainable. Naturally, this is going to leave you frustrated and despondent too. It's good to challenge yourself, but if you're always aiming for things that are incredibly difficult to achieve, even with a lot of effort, chances are you'll fall short.

You can also make the error of mistaking happiness for excitement— that feeling you get when people praise you or when you achieve certain things. Of course, there's nothing wrong with striving for what you want, but you shouldn't mistake these feelings for happiness. A lot of stress and anxiety comes from constantly needing that new high to feel good. It's not sustainable.

Ultimately, true happiness is an inside job and it's that calm feeling of inner peace. That feeling of knowing you're okay even when things are going badly. It's good to remind yourself of this when things aren't going your way. In the same way that a positive feeling, such as elation from a job promotion or falling in love, won't last forever, the same applies to negative feelings. They always pass, and that can be comforting to remember.

Like the weather, good and bad emotions come and go. You need to learn to embrace them, accept the moment and know that you're enough no matter what. Everyone deserves to be happy — no excuses.

An equation for happiness

I believe the key to happiness is to set micro goals that are achievable and that teach you to enjoy the daily process of achieving your goal. For example, if you want to run a marathon, you'll become overwhelmed if you set out to try and run 42 kilometres on day one. Instead, if you forget about the end goal and aim to run for 30 minutes a few times a week, you're more likely to stick to it and feel good about yourself in the process.

Further to that, if you not only set a goal to run a marathon, but also wanted to get the world record, chances are, no matter how hard you try, you will fall short of this goal. If, instead, you set the goal of running the best possible time you can and then try to beat that time in your second marathon, you're much more likely to achieve your goal and feel good about yourself.

To summarise, your aim should be to challenge yourself, enjoy the daily process and set small, attainable goals. Once you achieve these, you can raise the bar and challenge yourself with the next goal and so on. The big picture may or may not happen and is irrelevant. The important thing is to focus on the enjoying part right now, which is what mindfulness and meditation are all about.

Many people have talked about the happiness formula, which is expressed as:

$$Happiness = Reality - Expectations$$

If you expect one thing, and the reality is drastically different, you'll be disappointed. However, if your expectations are similar to reality, you'll be content. This can even be applied to bad situations. If something difficult or negative is happening and you expect the worst, and the reality is close to that, you'll be okay with it.

Again, I'm not saying that you shouldn't have big dreams, challenge yourself or aim high. The point is about managing the process. Life is a long game and if you only have a short-term view or aren't smart with how you challenge yourself, you'll be likely to burn out and give up before you've given your dreams a chance.

If you can break it down into small goals, enjoy the process and have low expectations, you can't lose. And if that big-picture goal does happen—even if it's as crazy as winning a world marathon record—it'll be a nice bonus. The key is that your self-worth isn't based on external events. You need to be able to feed yourself internally.

Move Your Mind with Nick: Check in

There are endless examples of how you can reframe your thinking. You'll see in the worksheets some activities with tools to help you build self-esteem and reframe how you get better at observing, how you view both gratitude and failure, and then how it's okay to not be okay. Try them out and keep coming back to apply them for new challenges!

DAILY GRATITUDE JOURNAL

Daily gratitude journalling is an incredibly powerful tool to re-wire your brain into looking for positives.

To get started, write down three things you are grateful for today.
(you can also write in a notepad, on your phone or anywhere else)

1 ....

2 ....

3 ....

The key is to repeat this each day. If you do this for 21 days or more, it will start to become a habit. Use the 21-Day Habit Tracker (see p. 223) to mark your daily progress. To take the next step in building this new habit, note your three things for days 2 and 3 below.

Day 2

1 ....

2 ....

3 ....

Day 3

1 ....

2 ....

3 ....

Like any other skill, the more we practise gratitude, the easier it will become. This simple practice can make a profound difference to your life.

DAILY GRATITUDE JOURNAL EXTRA

Here are just a few things to get you started. Create your own list, with everything you're grateful for.

Today I am grateful for my ...

Family because ....

....

Friends because ....

....

Career because ....

....

Body because ....

....

Past because ....

....

This moment because ....

....

My birth because ....

....

WEEKLY **OBSERVATIONS**

Use this weekly observations chart to reflect on your short-term progress, your patterns of commitment and your feelings about yourself. You can also use it to reward yourself for what went well and make notes about what you can improve for next time.

Week of:

What was positive about this week?	*What did not go to plan this week?*
☐	☐ ....
☐	☐ ....
☐	☐ ....
☐	☐ ....

Why did it go well?

....

....

What did I learn?

....

....

What do I want to improve on?

....

....

I am grateful for:

....

....

MONTHLY OBSERVATIONS

Use this monthly observations chart to reflect on your long-term progress, your patterns of commitment and your feelings about yourself. You can also use it to reward yourself for what went well and to make notes about what you can improve for next time.

Month of:

What was positive about this month?

☐ ....

☐ ....

☐ ....

☐ ....

What did not go to plan this month?

☐ ....

☐ ....

☐ ....

☐ ....

Why did it go well?

....

....

What did I learn?

....

....

What do I want to improve on?

....

....

I am grateful for:

....

....

REFRAMING 'FAILURE'

Life is a roller-coaster. We cannot control everything, and we are usually left burned-out and upset when we try to. We need to learn that in life, there is no such thing as 'failure'. We either get our desired outcome or we gain wisdom through our experience.

Approach every situation with the mindset that:

I AM GOING TO EITHER GET THE RESULT I WANT, OR LEARN FROM MY EXPERIENCE.

Life rarely unfolds as we plan, but if we can face it head-on, we are likely to get to where we want to, in one way or another, no matter how many unexpected obstacles we have to navigate.

Remember, if you practise every day for 21 days or more, you are likely to create a new habit!

Make a list of situations, events, relationships and anything else that did not go to plan:

What did you learn? What will you do differently? Did you gain new skills?

IT IS OK NOT TO BE OK!

Build your self-awareness with this daily 'check-in'.

Ask yourself:

1 On a scale of 1 (not at all) to 10 (absolutely), how comfortable am I being open, truthful and seen for who I am?

2 Do I hold back my emotion? When? In front of who? And how does this affect my life?

3 What gets in the way of being my most authentic self? What do I think I'm putting at risk by being authentic?

4 What fears hold me back, in general?

5 Do I want to be braver? When? And why will I benefit?

Nick's Tip:
Be honest with yourself. There are no right or wrong answers, only useful information. We need to realise that no-one is perfect and remember that there is no such thing as being complete. We are all a person in progress!

CONCLUSION

I just didn't know any better.

Six words. That's how I started this book, and now, how I'll end it.

They're small words that have taken me on a big journey, starting from as far back as I can remember.

They sum up what I suspect many others of my generation have felt at one point or another: loneliness, extreme anxiety, battles with depression and crippling terror.

My experiences were no fault of my own, nor of my upbringing, nor of my family. I simply lacked the tools or knowledge to understand what was happening in my body, and what was going on in my head. I needed help to navigate life through the lens of some really challenging mental health issues.

As I detailed in the introduction to the book, my obsessions led to depression and self-destruction. After a lot of soul searching, and help from friends, family and professionals, I started taking small steps to get my life back on track. I had no idea what I wanted or what I cared about. I just kept putting one foot in front of the other. It was a slow process in the beginning, but it opened a growth mindset and I started throwing myself at everything put in front of me using the habit formation techniques I've described in this book. I pushed myself to overcome insecurities and move out of my comfort zone, eventually gaining momentum as I confronted fears and tried new things and exciting experiences.

Had I not used consistent habits like practising public speaking at university, I would never have become comfortable and eventually transformed my fear into a career. If I could overcome a fear so deep that I would vomit each time I stood in front of people and push myself to front up time and again, then I could overcome anything.

Had that lesson not been burned so powerfully into my mind, I would never have danced on national television and gone on to speak publicly about my battle with mental health. I wouldn't have started running seminars and finding my life passion of making global change in mental health.

Had I not thrown myself into every challenge, putting myself in social situations and using acting to grow emotionally, I also wouldn't have found my other life goal of a career in film. It's a far cry from someone who couldn't even read out two lines in front of one person. No matter how much fear I felt, I lived by my mantra that if I could stick it out long enough, eventually something would give and improve.

Essentially, I learned through hardship, trial and error to create my own daily routine that helps me keep on top of my mental wellbeing and thrive. It's personal to me and one of the most important things in my life. And like everything, it takes hard work to master my mental health across every area of my life.

I set a big-picture life goal, and around that I have micro goals that keep changing and adapting. My vehicle is the art of creating habits, which is possibly the single most important factor in my journey of growth. Creating habits requires discipline and focus and teaches you the value of sticking things out. It forces you to try and enjoy the process and stay in it for the long haul. It changes your mindset from wanting instant gratification to enjoying the grind and finding deep meaning in achieving things you've had to work hard for.

I have always encouraged people to look at helping others in this way. The simple fact is that when you do things to help others, it makes you feel amazing. I still haven't found a better feeling than standing in front of hundreds, sometimes thousands, of people and speaking from the heart. Having people come up to you and reach out afterwards about how much it helped them is a truly incredible feeling. And it helps you too. It makes you want to do more of it. I say enjoy that feeling. Use it as motivation to do things, big or small, to help others. Be selfish and help others to help yourself. It will leave you feeling amazing and it may just change someone's life ... or save their life.

My hope is that in the future we don't have to re-educate people about mental health. It should be part of our daily learnings, taught to us through parenting, schooling and in organisations. It should be part of the daily conversation, seen in the exact same way that we see physical issues that are tangible, such as diabetes, obesity and cancer.

And it should start at school. Mental health education needs to become embedded in the schooling system, like any other subject. It should be taught in the same way as we learn English, mathematics and history, replacing an archaic education system in need of a major overhaul as part of skillsets required to function in the world.

Shouldn't it be a priority to learn how to think for ourselves, create and implement daily health habits, communicate, nurture healthy relationships and become more self-aware? We also need to educate the current generation so that they can educate their children—and parents and grandparents. To break the pattern passed on from generation to generation.

As for mental health, why should we wait for a catastrophic world event like COVID-19 to sit up and make change? In fact, we've already waited too long. With one person committing suicide around the world every 40 seconds, and depression affecting more than 264 million people around the globe, the writing is on the wall.

Above all else, I don't believe we will make broad, long-term change unless we view things in a preventative way. If I had learned these skills early on, I would have saved myself a lot of heartache. I would have avoided having to use trial and error to find solutions.

But as I said earlier, there's no one size fits all and we all react, learn and behave in different ways. Privileged or poor, mental health doesn't discriminate—as evidenced by the incredible mix of people who shared their stories on these pages.

As you finish this book, I want you to appreciate that when it comes to mental health, as in all other areas of life, there is no silver bullet. No one thing is going to make you change overnight. As in all areas of life, it takes daily work, discipline and focus to get results.

I've written this book as a tool and guide to help you find your own unique and sustainable way to improve your wellbeing. You don't have to do everything at once—just get started, and start small. Then, take things up a notch and set yourself up for success with continual monitoring and improvement. This will set you up for a life of integrity, discipline, meaning and purpose.

I can't recommend mastering this highly enough. Teach and discipline yourself to create habits in all facets of life and you will make lifelong change. And nothing would make me happier than to see you utilise this resource to achieve your potential.

I really hope that by reading this book, learning from the stories, and applying the lessons and tools in your own life, you too can achieve long-term change and inner peace. If you commit, stay resilient and apply discipline in creating long-term habits, nothing will stop you.

Here's to Moving Your Mind!

INDEX

raw whole foods 129

real connection, power
of 140–141

real friends 141

re-framing
—failure 239
—when fearful 231–232

rejection 35–36

relationship 151–153

relationships
—author's 156
—choosing healthy
214–215

relevant goals 204

resilience
—building 219–220
—Hugh Van
Cuylenberg on 72–73
—practising 75

Rob, Aunty, as emotional
confidant 147–148

routine, changing 50–51

routine and exercise 100

Schwass, Wayne, on holistic
health 77–80

screen time, halving 157

self
—building team around
50–51
—looking after 74
—putting first 39
—understanding 65–66

self-awareness
—daily check-in for 240
—developing 62

self-love 142

shame 131–132

sharing with others 81

shyness, author's 11, 155

sleep
—benefits of 173–174
—Dr Carmel Harrington
on 177–181
—getting enough 175–176
—keeping regular 164
—and mental health 175
—and mindfulness 164
—myths and miscon-
ceptions 179
—need for more 134
—preparing for 180–181
—prioritising 78–79

slowing down, challenge of 100

small, starting 94

small things, focussing on 66

smoothies 134

social media, addiction to 69–71

social platforms, addiction to 25

space, giving people 76

speaking, and business
course 10–12

specific goals 203

Stallone, Sylvester, and
perseverance 182–183

starting small 94

Printed and bound by CPI Group (UK) Ltd, Croydon, CR0 4YY
09/08/2021

03078622-0001

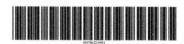